𝕮𝖆𝖒𝖇𝖗𝖎𝖉𝖌𝖊 𝕳𝖎𝖘𝖙𝖔𝖗𝖎𝖈𝖆𝖑 𝕾𝖊𝖗𝖎𝖊𝖘

EDITED BY G. W. PROTHERO, LITT.D., LL.D.

HONORARY FELLOW OF KING'S COLLEGE, CAMBRIDGE,
FORMERLY PROFESSOR OF HISTORY IN THE UNIVERSITY OF EDINBURGH.

WESTERN CIVILIZATION

IN ITS ECONOMIC ASPECTS

(ANCIENT TIMES)

London: C. J. CLAY AND SONS,
CAMBRIDGE UNIVERSITY PRESS WAREHOUSE,
AVE MARIA LANE.
Glasgow: 50, WELLINGTON STREET.

Leipzig: F. A. BROCKHAUS.
New York: THE MACMILLAN COMPANY.
Bombay and Calcutta: MACMILLAN AND CO., Ltd.

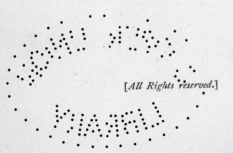

AN ESSAY

ON

WESTERN CIVILIZATION

IN ITS ECONOMIC ASPECTS

(ANCIENT TIMES)

BY

W. CUNNINGHAM, D.D.

HON. LL.D. EDIN.; HON. FELLOW OF GONVILLE AND CAIUS COLLEGE,
FELLOW AND LECTURER OF TRINITY COLLEGE, AND
VICAR OF GREAT S. MARY'S, CAMBRIDGE.

STEREOTYPED EDITION

CAMBRIDGE.
AT THE UNIVERSITY PRESS.
1902

4347 2

First Edition 1898.   *Reprinted* 1902.

PREFACE.

IT has been my endeavour in this essay to bring out the main economic features in the growth and diffusion of the Civilized Life in Western Europe, to which so many peoples and countries have contributed; I have not aimed at portraying the development of each of the separate polities to which reference is made.

Some of the difficulties that have to be faced, in engaging in such a task, have been obvious from the first, and others have been felt more clearly as the work progressed. The chief of these is due to the lack of information. The social and economic side of life was so familiar to their contemporaries, and was often so uneventful, that chroniclers have rarely thought it worth while to describe it particularly. We have to depend on incidental remark, rather than on detailed and deliberate description. This silence is especially perplexing in early times, and renders it very difficult for us to trace the precise connection between one primitive civilization and another. We have often to be content with establishing the fact of intercourse, and thus indicating a line along which certain arts and habits could be easily transmitted. It is of course possible that some art or institution may have been invented independently in different societies; but so many ages and peoples have been and are unenterprising and uninventive, that, in the case of distant but related societies, transmission along lines of known intercourse always seems a more probable hypothesis than that of independent origination.

But there is another difficulty; even when distinct information on some economic topic has been recorded, we have not sufficient knowledge of the circumstances to be able to interpret the evidence with confidence. The last word has not been said on the precise aims of Solon's legislation, nor on the exact character of the leather money of the Carthaginians, nor on the agrarian system of the Germans in the time of Tacitus.

Perhaps the hardest task of all is to find suitable phraseology in which to describe and discuss the reported phenomena. Before the era of money-economy, the sides of life, which we distinguish as economic and as political, were merged together; in Egyptian history, foreign commerce cannot be readily distinguished from tribute paid by dependencies, and (to use modern terms) the "organization of labour" was intimately connected with the "incidence of taxation." In Greek and Roman life, analysis is much simpler, and modern economic categories—such as capital—can be usefully applied.

Many of the remarks in the following pages are necessarily of a tentative character; I cannot but hope, however, that the advance of Economic Knowledge will gradually give us the means of applying appropriate conceptions to all the various phases of industrial life, however unlike they may be to our own, and that the masses of new material, which research and excavation may supply, will fill up many of the *lacunae* in our information regarding past ages.

I am much indebted for suggestions and advice to Professor Prothero and Professor Ridgeway, also to Dr Jackson and Mr Wyse, Fellows of Trinity College, and Mr G. Townsend Warner, formerly Fellow of Jesus College. Mr H. J. Edwards of Selwyn has been so kind as to read the whole work both in manuscript and in proof; he has also constructed the chronological chart and supplied the maps for the volume.

W. C.

TRINITY COLLEGE, CAMBRIDGE,
12 *February*, 1898.

Advantage has been taken of the opportunity afforded by a demand for a fresh issue to introduce a few verbal emendations, but it has not seemed desirable to make any substantial alterations or additions.

W. C.

12 *March*, 1902.

TABLE OF CONTENTS.

INTRODUCTION.

BOOK I.

THE PRECURSORS.

CHAPTER I.

EGYPT.

CHAPTER II.

Judaea.

CHAPTER III.

The Phoenicians.

BOOK II.

The Greeks.

CHAPTER I.

Greece as connected with Phoenicia and Egypt.

CHAPTER II.

City Life.

CHAPTER III.

ALEXANDER'S EMPIRE AND THE HELLENISTIC PERIOD.

BOOK III.

THE ROMANS.

CHAPTER I.

THE STRUGGLE FOR SUPREMACY IN THE WEST.

CHAPTER II.

THE ROMAN REPUBLIC.

CHAPTER III.

THE ROMAN EMPIRE.

CHAPTER IV.

CONSTANTINOPLE.

MAPS.

WESTERN CIVILIZATION IN ITS ECONOMIC ASPECTS.

INTRODUCTION.

ANCIENT TIMES.

1. THERE is a great interest in disinterring the vestiges of an ancient and forgotten civilization. The ruined cities of Central America or of Mashona- *Isolation and Intercourse.* land bear witness to the existence, in some former time, of a cultivated race which had made considerable progress in the arts of life. These men have wholly disappeared, and antiquaries dispute as to their racial affinities, the sources of their prosperity, and the reasons of their fall. Part of the romance which lends attraction to such investigations arises from the apparent isolation of each of these communities, and from the obscurity which shrouds alike their origin and extinction. In dealing with Western Civilization, this element of romance is almost entirely wanting; one great civilization after another has risen and has waned in the Mediterranean lands, but each has been linked in the closest fashion with those that preceded it, and has in turn brought influences of many kinds to bear on those that arose subsequently. We have no apparent isolation, but constant interconnection and frequent intercourse;

our main business in trying to follow the story is to set ourselves to detect and to trace the points of contact between
different communities, and the influence which each has owed
to, or has exercised upon, the others.

In the lands that encircle the Mediterranean there has
been an unbroken tradition of civilized life from the earliest
times; it has shifted from point to point, from Egypt to Phoenicia, from Phoenicia and Carthage to Greece and Rome, from
Constantinople to Italy and France. The life has been more
vigorous at some periods than at others; at times it has been
circumscribed, and again it has spread abroad to affect the
destinies of distant peoples. It has never died out or become
extinct. The English nation, which has been the principal
agent in diffusing the influence of Western Civilization throughout the East, has received a great heritage of industrial skill
and commercial enterprise from other peoples. If we would
understand aright the part our country has played and is playing in the world, we must try to understand how this great
heritage of industrial and commercial activity has been built
up—in what fashion each people has inherited and perpetuated
the tradition it received, and what contribution each has added
of its own.

2. When the nature of the subject is thus stated, we may
see that a very large field of interesting enquiry
is excluded from the scope of our investigation.
When we discuss the influence which one people exercises on
another and the intercourse between them, we are thinking
exclusively of the peoples which have so far advanced as to
settle in a definite territory and to attain a considerable degree
of social organisation; many tribes have never reached this
social condition. Men who are more or less migratory in
habits, and depend for their livelihood on hunting or fishing,
or upon the herds which roam over large tracts of country,
may have considerable skill, and make much advance in the
industrial arts; they may engage to a considerable extent in

commerce, and they must have some forms of family or tribal organisation. But they do not build up a prosperous civilization; ranging as they do from place to place, they cannot accumulate the stores of wealth which provide the opportunity for devoting attention to literature and art[1]. They accept the provision which nature affords, but they do not set themselves to overcome the obstacles which hem in the path of material progress[2]. We are only concerned at present with the peoples which have already settled down to agricultural life, or built themselves cities as centres for industry and depôts for commerce; the steps by which any group of tribes attained this condition may be of the greatest interest, but they hardly fall within the scope of history.

3. There are different ways in which intercourse between two peoples may arise. The most obvious modes of contact have their origin in connection with war and with commerce. Since hostile and friendly intercourse appear to be very distinct indeed, it is curious to notice how closely war and commerce have been inter-connected. In primitive ages the two can hardly be distinguished, and we find the two ideas blended in the Homeric poems. At a later date the Viking who went out to plunder might incidentally turn his hand to trade; when he brought the captives taken in war to be sold at a slave mart he was betaking himself to commerce. Even when the two are distinct, they are closely connected; for war may open up new points for commerce, as was done by the Crusades, and a successful war may give securities for peaceful commerce; on the other hand, commercial rivalries have often occasioned the

Hostile and Friendly Intercourse.

---

[1] Compare Aristotle, *Metaphysics* A. c. i. § 11, on the importance of leisure as an element in social well-being, and as giving the opportunity for intellectual progress. For a more modern discussion of the same topic see Bagehot, *Physics and Politics*, 71—73. He dwells on the influence of slavery in making leisure possible.

[2] Cunningham, *Growth of English History and Commerce*, I. p. 35.

outbreak of hostilities between nations. War and commerce
are very different indeed, in the manner in which they react
respectively on agriculture and industry; but both modes of
intercourse have had much to do with the diffusion of industrial
and commercial skill.

4. It is at all events clear that the effect of a successful
war, which establishes any wide-spread political
influence, supplies the conditions of easy intercommunication. Where there are many separate
tribes or cities with frequently changing relations
between them, there must be elements of insecurity and uncertainty which are not favourable to regular commerce. On
the other hand the establishment of a wide empire on land, or
of sovereignty by sea, gives the opportunity for peaceful commerce to arise, and it may do much more to promote it.
Under the Roman Empire the resources of the provinces were
developed so that they might serve as granaries for the capital;
new fauna and flora were acclimatised in distant regions; and
deliberate efforts were made to open up conquered provinces
by great roads which could be used for military and for commercial communications alike. At a later time, the wave of
Mohammedan conquest served to give the conditions under
which a knowledge of the arts and sciences of the East might
be cultivated in remote parts of the West, where civilization
had been almost entirely destroyed by a succession of barbarian
invasions.

Besides the direct influence exercised by conquerors, there
may sometimes be a curious transference of skill from the
conquered[1]. Rome learned much from the Greek cities she
overthrew[2], and the commerce of the Empire was largely carried

*Social Con-
ditions—Con-
quest, Factor-
ies, Colonies.*

---

[1] On the influence of Syrian prisoners of war on Egyptian arts see
Flinders Petrie, *History*, II. 147. The diffusion of religious ideas through
the agency of captives has been of not infrequent occurrence. Cf. 2 Kings
v. 4. Also in Ireland; Montalembert, *Monks of the West*, II. 390.

[2] Graecia capta ferum victorem cepit, Hor. *Ep.* II. i. 156.

on by Greek slaves, or persons of Greek extraction. In our own island it appears that the conquered Britons left some mark on the household employments of the Angles who conquered them; and on the Continent at all events, the influence of the conquered Roman on the conquering barbarian was very decided, though not always wholesome[1].

Commercial intercourse arises not only between different parts of the same empire, but between regions which have no direct political connections; if it is to be regular and constant, however, the two trading parties must come to some kind of understanding as to the terms on which they meet and do business together. In modern times there are ample facilities for intercourse between all civilized nations, and consuls who see to the interests of their countrymen are found in every important town. Even with half-civilized peoples there are treaty rights, by which trading privileges are secured. In ancient times it was more common for the men of one city to secure a factory at a distant port, and thus to have a guaranteed footing in the foreign town or district. Similarly a great deal of the mercantile business of medieval times was carried on by aliens temporarily resident in some specially reserved part of a city, and subject to special burdens, though secured in definite privileges and immunities in their own quarters; these immigrants had not a little to do with the transmission both of articles of merchandise and of the arts of industry.

Where settlements were made, not in an active commercial centre, but in a land of which the resources were imperfectly developed, they may be regarded not so much as factories, but as colonies. There were many important differences between the colonies of the ancient and of the modern world, and even between the colonies of the Phoenicians and of the Greek peoples; but such settlements have in all ages served as centres where the people of some land found hospitable

[1] Montalembert, *Monks of the West*, II. 229.

reception, so that regular trade between them and the mother country was possible. The distribution of the Phoenician and Greek colonies in the Mediterranean marked out the spheres where these rival traders exercised an influence, when neither the one nor the other was strong enough to maintain an effective sovereignty on the sea.

5. Such are the social conditions under which commercial intercourse has most commonly occurred; but it is also necessary to remember that it must have a physical basis. If its communications are good, a great political power may be able to draw to itself the products of other lands as the result of a sort of taxation; but in an ordinary way, there must be a give and take in commercial intercourse. Distant lands are sought out by traders, because of some valued product which can be obtained in the course of trade; and the commercial importance of a country depends on the nature of the commodities it can offer in exchange to the people of other lands. It may have some natural product to give, as Cornwall afforded tin and Spain silver in the ancient times; as Egypt and Sicily provided corn; and the ports of the Black Sea fish. It may be a manufacturing centre[1], as Tyre was at one period and Corinth at another, and supply textile fabrics that are in great request. Or it may be a depot on a great commercial route, where the products and manufactures of distant places are stored and are readily procurable. Antioch and Alexandria, Carthage and Marseilles were commercial cities of the last named type.

Physical Bases—Products, Manufactures, Goods.

It is obvious that any of these sources of national prosperity may fail, and that the community which depends on

---

[1] Early success in manufactures seems to depend more closely on personal aptitudes than on physical conditions, and it is not always easy to account for the localisation of particular trades in particular places. At the same time the possession of the materials requisite for some manufacture, and in modern times of facilities for mechanical power, either coal or water, have exerted considerable influence.

them may in consequence decay. Mines are sure to be exhausted sooner or later; and the veins of silver ore at Laurium and in Spain have lost their importance. Changes of climate may render a fertile region barren, or the soil may be exhausted by long-continued cultivation. Manufacturing preeminence may be sapped by a failure of materials, or by the successful development of rival industries in more favourable positions. On the other hand, owing to the progress of discovery or to gradual physical processes, like the silting up of a channel, there may be great alterations in trade routes; progress in the art of ship-building and the introduction of steamboats and railways have revolutionised the modes of communication. We see the effects of these changes on a small scale in the case of some English towns, such as Lynn or Boston, that were important in the Middle Ages, and have had little share in the recent developments of English commerce; Venice and Bruges are still more striking examples. Trade routes, depending as they do on physical conditions, are wonderfully permanent, and even when temporarily closed by social or political incidents[1] they are likely to be reopened; but yet there are elements of change and uncertainty in regard to them. It is probable that the countries which are able to supply some natural product, like corn, in considerable quantities, are those which have the firmest physical basis for the maintenance of their material prosperity. The long-continued importance of Egypt in the commercial world is primarily due to the regular inundations which replenish the soil and maintain its fertility for the production of grain and cotton.

6. In endeavouring to survey this large field, we must try to discriminate the principal landmarks. It is our object to see how each of the great peoples of the past has supplied its quota to that Western Civilization which is being so

Tokens of the highest material prosperity of each civilization.

---

[1] As the routes to the East were interrupted by the rise of the Moham-

rapidly diffused over the whole globe at the present time; we want to detect the special contribution of each. This we are most likely to observe, if we try to examine the condition of each country or people at the epoch when it had attained its highest point of industrial and commercial prosperity. As we approach each civilization in turn we shall be able to describe what was available from its predecessors; we can see what were the characteristic features of the economic life of that people, and what new bent it gave, at the zenith of its greatness, to the energies of our race.

Wealth and power are so closely interconnected that it might seem at first sight as if the periods when any people attained to the highest pitch of political power would also be those of greatest interest economically. Yet there have been flourishing cities which did an enormous trade, but which never attained to the first rank as political powers; and in some cases political ambition has been sacrificed for the sake of commercial advantage. There is a better test and a more obvious token of great material prosperity; in any community where there is wealth to spare, which can be sunk in magnificent buildings or other public works, there is a permanent record of its greatness or of the riches of its rulers. On the whole, the period when the characteristic buildings of each civilization were erected was the time of its greatest material prosperity; this gives us the means of gauging most definitely the precise nature of its contribution to the growth of Western Civilization as a whole.

7. A very few words may now suffice to indicate the **Plan and Divisions.** nature of the plan which will be pursued in the following pages. The sources of Western Civilization are to be found in (1) Egypt, and Phoenicia; the characteristic features of each of these ancient civilizations, so marvellous in themselves and so striking in their

medan powers; and the great highway from Marseilles to the North was rendered impracticable by the Hundred Years' War.

contrasts with one another, will occupy us first of all. Without dwelling at length on the difficult problems as to the precise channels by which civilization travelled in these early days, we shall turn to (2) the Greeks and the Greek colonies; we shall see how deeply they were indebted to their predecessors and how rapidly they outstripped them. The development of Greek civilization was followed by its diffusion through the conquests of Alexander and his generals on the one side, and on the other by (3) the action of the Romans, when they had at length emerged successfully from their rivalry with the Phoenician colonies at Carthage. The incursions of the barbarians gradually circumscribed the area of civilized life in the West, and forced it to centre more and more in the dependencies of the New Rome which Constantinê had founded; but even where the barbarians seemed most ruthless, some elements of the old civilization remained here and there, and these were gradually reinvigorated as Christian Rome rose from the ruins to guide the destinies of the West.

These are the main divisions, which we must take in turn; and in dealing with each of them we must look with special care at the physical features as well as the political conditions which helped to assign to each country its special part. For physical conditions are of importance not only in the rise, but in the decline and fall of nations. When we have succeeded in marking the influence which each civilization was able to exercise on the subsequent history of the world, we shall have the more melancholy interest of examining the reasons which account for its decay.

BOOK I.

CHAPTER I.

EGYPT.

8. THE destinies of a country are affected in many ways
Physical Features. by its physical features[1], and there is no civilization of which this is more obviously true than of that which arose in the land of Egypt. To Greek eyes[2], as to our own[3], it was a country which abounded in the strangest paradoxes; there is something abnormal even in the simple fact that its material prosperity depends absolutely and entirely upon a river. Through the barren sands of a valley guarded by rugged hills the Nile has ploughed its course; year by year it has brought down a deposit of alluvial soil; as this has accumulated in the Delta, a larger area of rich land has been built up on a region once washed by the sea. A narrow strip along the river banks together with the Delta and other lands of Lower Egypt are the only fertile parts of the country; but for these, the maintenance of a large population and the building up of a great civilization would have been impossible; and they are, in their origin, the gift of the river.

More than this, continual cultivation would be impossible, in the dry Egyptian climate where rain rarely falls, if it were

---

[1] Physical conditions offer obstacles which hinder the development of a race in some given direction—but these obstacles are not always insuperable. Cunningham, *Growth of Industry and Commerce*, I. 13.

[2] Herodotus, II. 35.   [3] Milner, *England in Egypt*, 3.

not for the supply of water furnished by the annual rising of the Nile. It is the great event of the year, presaged by curious changes in the colour of the water, and a gradual increase in its volume, till it serves to reach the channels from which the irrigation of the country is carried on. The rising is watched with the greatest anxiety; should it fall short of the usual amount, there is sure to be at least a partial failure of crops; should it rise too high there is a danger of disastrous floods.

Hence it is necessary for the very existence of the country that the river on which so much depends should be wisely controlled. Of Egypt it is true that the physical conditions, which have rendered its civilization possible, are not natural, but artificial. Mena, who reigned as Pharaoh about 4777 B.C. and founded the dynasty which is generally reckoned as the first, undertook a great engineering work, which may be said to have rendered Lower Egypt what it is. Herodotus, a witness who stands much nearer to our day than to the time of the building of the great dyke, thus relates the tradition in regard to this work. "The Priests stated that Mena, the first that ever ruled over Egypt, threw up in the first place the dyke that protects Memphis; for previously the whole of the stream flowed along the sand-covered mountain ridge fronting Libya; but Mena, beginning about one hundred stadia above Memphis, filled in the elbow made by the Nile to the South : and thus not only exhausted the old bed, but formed also a canal by which the river was made to flow in the mid-space between the mountains. Even at the present day this ancient elbow, repelling the Nile in his course, is attended to and watched with great care by the Persians, and fortified every year with additional works, for should the river rise over and burst this dyke, the whole of Memphis would be exposed to the danger of being swept away[1]." This ancient work is still maintained with the same

---

[1] Herodotus, II. 99 (Laurent).

care by English engineers[1]; like other great engineering works
on the Nile it serves a double purpose, for it both protects
certain low-lying lands from flood, and gives facilities for
directing the water into reservoirs and channels which may
be used for irrigation.

To the river the alluvial soil in Egypt owes its origin; and
the river, duly controlled, supplies water for cultivating it;
the river also is the great means for internal communication
and trade. It seems that the camel was unknown in the
earliest period of Egyptian greatness, and land transport was
little used; the river, however, gave ample opportunities for
the conveyance of goods through the length of the land; and
it had no breadth. By means of water-carriage vast masses
of granite could be transported from the rocks at Assouan to
construct buildings and monuments, and goods of every kind
seem to have followed the same routes. In fact it seems as
if in the Old Empire any other mode of travelling than by
water was practically unknown[2].

It is not easy to account satisfactorily for the mineral
wealth of the ancient Egyptians; they were acquainted with
iron, tin, copper and gold; but none of these except gold is
believed to have been found within Egypt itself[3]. Additional
supplies of this precious metal could be procured far up the
Nile valley in Nubia; and copper was found in the Sinaitic
Peninsula, a district where the Pharaohs soon asserted their
sway. The sources of their tin and iron are not definitely
known[3]; the latter metal was apparently not available in large
quantities in the Old Empire, and most of the implements
were made of bronze.

Another of the physical conditions of Egypt, which has
been important in every age, is of special interest to the
historian. The warm, dry climate is favourable to tillage,

[1] Milner, *England in Egypt*, 276, 280.
[2] Erman, *Life in Ancient Egypt*, 479.
[3] *Ibid.* 462.

but it has also rendered possible the preservation of records from the very earliest times; we know far more of life in Ancient Egypt than we do of many civilizations which lie much nearer to us in point of time. Of the Hittites, Phrygians, and the peoples of Asia Minor, the remains are so slight that it is difficult to describe their affinities or to assign them their due place in the development of the Western World. From Egypt we have a vast mass of monumental works and relics: and what is far more important, the archaeological remains can be interpreted in the light of numerous inscriptions and literary remains which the climate has permitted to survive. The fulness of our knowledge enables us to see with clearness the high condition to which Egypt had advanced in the most distant times and to feel how deep is the debt which all subsequent civilization owes to her.

From the foregoing account of these physical characteristics we plainly see what were the principal limitations and opportunities which helped to determine the industrial and social life of the Egyptians. In the earliest times of all, Lower Egypt was chiefly available for pasturage, and cattle-herding and wool-growing were much encouraged. As time advanced however the land was reclaimed, much as the Cambridgeshire fens have been, and adapted to tillage instead, and the opportunities for pastoral life became more restricted. At the time of the New Empire the land of Goshen[1], on the extreme east of Lower Egypt, was not yet adapted for cultivation, and it was in this region that the Israelites were settled. The increasing facilities for tillage rendered Egypt more and more important as a corn-growing country.

It is clear too that Egypt was, to an unusual extent, a "self-sufficing" country. The monuments prove to us that

[1] Naville, *The Shrine of Saft-el-henneh* (Egypt Exploration Fund), p. 18.

industrial arts of every sort were highly developed under the
Old Empire, but there was no need to depend on other
peoples for the requisite materials. With flax and cotton
fibres, with abundant food, and ample materials for building,
Egypt was not compelled to go beyond her own borders for
any of the ordinary requirements of life. The mountains and
the deserts served on the whole to protect her from the incursions of enemies, and gave security for the prosecution of
the arts of peace, and there was little inducement to open
up friendly intercourse with other peoples. A country thus
self-sufficient had no need to engage in trade; it seems that
during the greater part of the Old Empire the Egyptians had
no foreign commerce at all[1], and that even in later days they
failed to develop much aptitude for it. That the Egyptians
were excellent watermen is certain; but they were never
attracted to engage habitually in distant maritime enterprise,
and were not dependent on it for their material prosperity.
A contrast has been drawn, in a preceding paragraph, between
the isolated civilizations of which relics survive in Africa and
America, and that Western civilization which has continued
to flourish through the intercourse of many peoples. This
Western civilization has its root, however, in the work of a
people which developed and elaborated a flourishing life of
its own, with but little actual intercourse with its neighbours.
We cannot say that all the varied skill which Egypt exhibited
in different arts of life was indigenous to the land, but at least

---

[1] Erman points out that there was, despite the lack of material, considerable skill in ship-building under the Old Empire (*Life in Ancient
Egypt*, 480). The want of harbours in the Delta, and the inaccessibility of
the harbours in the Red Sea, render it improbable that Egypt developed
maritime commerce at an early time (*Ib.*, p. 15). Maspero (*Dawn of
Civilization*, p. 392) argues from the presence of amber, iron and cedar in
the buildings of the pyramid age, that there must have been Mediterranean
commerce, and assumes, in opposition to the received opinion, that it was
conducted by the Egyptians themselves.

we have no means of tracing it to any earlier centre of civilized life[1].

9. The most striking feature of Egyptian history is its extraordinary duration; in the days of the "father of history" its story stretched back into a forgotten past. The Greek cities, as independent political communities, had in comparison but a momentary existence; the history of Rome, from the time of its foundation till the transference of the seat of government to Constantinople, covers more than a millennium— a period which corresponds to the history of the English monarchy from Egbert to the present time; but according to the most generally received chronology, the story of Egypt from the first to the last of the Pharaohs ranges over four thousand years. The list of the Pharaohs, arranged in dynasties, was compiled from authentic sources by Manetho; but it has been preserved in a very imperfect form, and there is grave difficulty in interpreting it, especially in discerning how far the dynasties were successive, or whether two or more reigned simultaneously in different parts of the country[2]. There are consequently considerable differences of opinion among scholars about the precise dating of particular occurrences, and about the lapse of time between one and another of the great crises in Egyptian history.

Periods of Material Prosperity.

These difficulties about chronology do not affect the accuracy of our knowledge in regard to the more prominent persons and events. The inscribed monuments raised by the Egyptians, and the other writings they left behind, give us a mighty mass of materials from which information may

---

[1] The Egyptians of the New Empire were indebted to Syrian peoples for many improvements in the Arts. Flinders Petrie, *History*, II. 146.

[2] This difficulty is specially felt with regard to the Hyksos and contemporary dynasties. On the whole subject of Egyptian chronology, and the ingenious confirmation of historical statements from astronomical data, see Flinders Petrie, *History*, I. 248.

be drawn. We may be mistaken in assigning a precise
position to any Pharaoh in the course of centuries, though
the advance of detailed knowledge is serving to eliminate
one source of confusion after another. In any case, however, there is evidence of undoubted authority which sets
before us many facts of Egyptian history and enables us to
understand their meaning and bearing so far as economic
affairs are concerned.

Egyptian history falls into four great periods, each of
which has left important monuments to testify of the greatness of successive Pharaohs. (1) The earliest period of all
—the Old Empire—was marked by the erection of the great
pyramids at Gizeh; Memphis was then the capital of the
country, and the most flourishing city of this period. We
cannot estimate how many generations had gone by before
this great civilization was built up; but Flinders Petrie dates
its close at 3335 B.C. (2) In the second great period—the
Middle Empire—we find the seat of government transferred
to Thebes; it is marked by successful public works in connection with Lake Moeris and the building of the Labyrinth.
It was terminated by an invasion of Shepherd Kings from
the East, who dominated the country for more than five
hundred years before they were expelled about 1600 B.C.
The expulsion was followed by (3) the greatest period of
Egyptian prosperity, under the New Empire; Thebes was
still the capital, and the most striking vestiges which remain
to us are the temples of Luxor and Karnak. During this
era Egypt was drawn out of her isolation, and became for
awhile a great conquering power, but the period of the
Exodus (circ. 1220 B.C.) marks her decline from this high position; she struggled, not always successfully, to hold her own
against rivals in the north-east, the west and the south.
(4) The fourth period of prosperity was but a temporary
revival, chiefly effected through the development of foreign
commerce carried on in foreign ships; it was fitting that

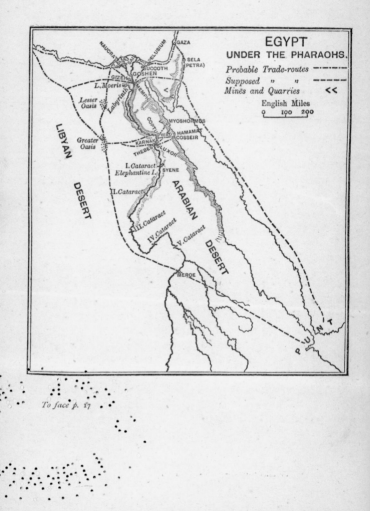

EGYPT
UNDER THE PHARAOHS.

Probable Trade-routes — · — · —
Supposed   "   "   — — — —
Mines and Quarries   <<

English Miles
0   100   200

NAUCRA
PELUSIUM
GAZA
SUCCOTH
GOSHEN
(SELA
(PETRA)
GIZEH
L. Moeris
Labyrinth
MEMPHIS
Lesser
Oasis
COPTOS
MYOSHORMOS
Greater
Oasis
HAMMAM
COSSEIR
KARNAK
THEBES
LUXOR
I. Cataract
Elephantine I.
SYENE
II. Cataract
LIBYAN
DESERT
III. Cataract
IV. Cataract
V. Cataract
ARABIAN
DESERT
MEROE
PUNT

To face p. 17

the capital should be once more transferred, and should be settled at the city of Sais, which gave more convenient access to Greek adventurers. The last period is of less importance in itself; but indirectly it has a high degree of interest, for it furnishes the most obvious link of connection between Egyptian and European civilization.

10. I. The three pyramids of Gizeh are the most striking monuments of the Old Empire; they are also remarkable in another way, since they seem in an extraordinary degree to bear witness to the industrial skill and social conditions of the people by whom they were reared. The carefully chosen sites and the peculiarities of their construction indicate, not obscurely, that the builders were well accustomed to observe and take account of the movements of the heavenly bodies. They must have had the means of maintaining and effectively organizing a vast army of labourers; there is little difficulty in identifying most of the materials, and fixing on the regions from which they were transported, while the accurate workmanship testifies to the skill with which they were wrought.

The Pyramids.

Even though these Egyptians may perhaps have been better provided with mechanical appliances[1] than is sometimes supposed, and even though water-carriage might be used in times of inundation to bring the blocks of syenite close to the site, the amount of human labour required must have been extraordinary. The tradition of the misery involved in the erection of the Great Pyramid was put on record by Herodotus. Cheops "ordered all the Egyptians to labour in his own service, some of whom he accordingly appointed to the task of dragging the blocks, from the quarries in the Arabian mountains, down to the Nile; others he stationed to take the said blocks, when brought across the river in vessels, and drag them to the ranges called the Libyan mountains. They

[1] Flinders Petrie, *Lecture on Arts of Ancient Egypt*, p. 26.

C. W. C.   2

were compelled to labour in this manner by one hundred thousand at a time, each party during three months[1]." Ten years were devoted to making a causeway which leads to the Pyramid and in executing subterranean works; while twenty years more were employed in building the Pyramid itself. Herodotus goes on to dwell on the enormous expense which must have been required to feed and clothe such an army of labourers, as well as to provide them with the necessary tools.

To meet this enormous outlay in labour and in expense, the Memphite Pharaohs were able to rely on the resources of forced labour and of regular taxation exacted from the produce of the soil. Tradition assigned to the builders of the two largest pyramids an evil pre-eminence in their reckless demands on the forced labour of their subjects[2]. For the work was not done by slaves, or only to a small extent; by far the heavier burden was borne by the Egyptian cultivators, who were not mere chattels. Their absolute subjection may perhaps be connected with the conditions under which Egyptian tillage was carried on; it was rendered possible by the great ramparts and canals which the Pharaohs had raised: the cultivators were the tenants of Pharaoh, who was the one supreme proprietor. It was essential to their very existence that they should occasionally give their labour to keep the banks and canals in order: and it was not unnatural that they should pay a rent or impost to Pharaoh according to the benefit which their lands derived from irrigation. It was only under a despotism that the rivalries of different villages could be held in check and the water supply turned to the best account[3]; but despotism, though inevitable, was not always

---

[1] Herodotus, II. 124.

[2] Flinders Petrie (*History*, I. 40) argues that sufficient labour could be obtained by pressing workmen during the three months of the year when, owing to the inundation of the Nile, they would otherwise have been idle.

[3] Maspero, *Dawn*, 70.

beneficent. The lands were carefully measured[1], and a portion
of the product, which was supposed to vary with the height of
the inundation and consequent benefit to the land, was exacted
from each. This careful survey, which was being constantly
revised, served in unscrupulous hands as an instrument of
intolerable tyranny. The assessment seems to have been so
high that the quotas of the cultivators could only be exacted
by beating, and those who failed to meet the demands put
upon them were compelled to work out the amount of their
debts in forced labour. Control of the food supply was the
basis of the Pharaohs' power, for it is fairly clear that it was
through the hold obtained upon the people by the great
irrigation works, that the Pharaohs were able to extort such
toil and wealth from the cultivating peasantry[2]. By controlling the river the Pharaohs had acquired political power,
and they used this political power to carry out the huge
buildings on which they had fixed their ambition.

In the use of political power as the instrument of exacting
and of controlling labour on this vast scale we have a curious
contrast with our own days[3]. There is much serious pressure
on the labourer to-day; with the misery caused by sweating
brought before us, we are apt to speak as if the poverty of
the overworked were entirely due to competition. Many of
us are inclined to argue that it would be well to substitute
organisation for our existing arrangements. In ancient Egypt,
so far as we see, there was no competition, and no speculation
or money-grubbing on the part of individuals. There was an
industrial tyranny which oppressed the labourer, and ground
the lives out of criminals in the mines; but this was merely
part of the administrative system of the country; the political

---

[1] Maspero, *Dawn*, 330. Lumbroso, *Recherches*, p. 289.

[2] The mass of the cultivators were in this position, though there were
also large estates cultivated by servile labour.

[3] Something similar survives in modern times in countries where there
is conscription.

and social organisation were not distinct[1]. Our present social arrangements may be faulty in many ways, but there is at least an opportunity of introducing correctives and palliatives in industrial life gradually, and without upsetting the whole fabric of society by a servile war.

11. II. A gap of something like a thousand years separated

Lake Moeris. the fourth dynasty, when the Pyramids were built, from the twelfth dynasty, when another group of public works of first-rate importance was carried out. A large area of fertile soil was reclaimed from Lake Moeris, which had extended over a natural depression to the west of Memphis, now known as the Fayum[2]; the communication with the Nile Valley was also improved, so that the diminished lake was converted into a sort of reservoir which was available for storing water to be used when the Nile was low. At the entrance to this Lake Moeris a huge building was erected, which was named Labyrinth[3] by the Greeks; it moved the admiration of travellers even more than the Pyramids themselves. Herodotus, who had himself visited it, says, "It exceeds all powers of description: for it is such that if we could collect together all the Hellenic edifices, all the works they have wrought, the collection would be evidently inferior as respects the labour employed and the expense incurred. The temple of Ephesus is undoubtedly magnificent, and so is that at Samos; the Pyramids likewise were noble structures, each equal to many of the mighty works achieved by the Hellenes put together, but the Labyrinth beats the Pyramids

---

[1] "Das Pharaonenreich ist bekanntlich gerade in seiner ältesten Gestalt, zur Zeit der Pyramidenerbauer, ein fest geordneter Beamtenstaat, ähnlich dem byzantinischen Reich, mit dem ganzen Apparat einer komplizierten Beamtenhierarchie und eines umständlichen schriftlichen Verfahrens." Meyer, *Die Wirthschaftliche Entwickelung des Alterthums*, p. 9.

[2] Flinders Petrie, *History*, I. 191.

[3] i.e. Lope-ro-hounit, or temple at the head of the lake. Maspero, *Histoire Ancienne*, 110.

themselves[1]." It has not, however, so successfully resisted the
ravages of time and of ruthless marauders, and few vestiges of
it remain, nor is it easy to gather the precise purpose it served.
Both Herodotus and Strabo agree, however, in connecting it
with the political organisation of the country; it was "composed of as many palaces as there were formerly *nomes*," or
districts, and the nomes assembled there for religious rites[2].
It serves to bring out one characteristic of the political condition of Egypt, which is not accentuated in the Pyramids;
for we cannot but regard the state as composed of great
feudatories, each of which in his own hereditary dominions
imitated on a smaller scale the works of Pharaoh and organised his estates on the royal model, while at the same time
he acted as an administrator on behalf of his royal master.
An inscription which commemorates the life of Ameny, one of
the feudal nobility under Usertesen I. (2758 B.C.), serves at least
to illustrate the duties of the good official of the time. He
managed the royal herds with exemplary honesty, and kept
back nothing for himself out of the royal workshops. And,
while honest towards his master, he was also "full of good-
ness and of a gentle character—a prince who loved his town."
He never afflicted the child of the poor or the widow: he
never disturbed any owner of lands. He brought the whole
of his district under cultivation and found food for the inhabitants, so that there were no hungry folk in his time even
in the years of famine[3]. At the same time it is only too
probable that if Ameny really possessed all the virtues he
claimed, he was a very exceptional personage. Another account gives a very different picture of the condition of the
Egyptians during this same period. Though they were not

---

[1] Herodotus, II. 148.

[2] Strabo XVII. 1. 3. Herodotus (II. 148) treats it as a building where
the representation of twelve (not thirty) confederate families was arranged
for.

[3] Brugsch, I. 137.

servile, and the artisans were organised in corporations[1], they were goaded to the most arduous labour in town and country alike. A scribe of the time congratulated himself on his good fortune as compared with that of the metal workers with wrinkled hands and protracted toil; or the stone workers and masons, who have hardly time to rest or to wash; or the weaver, who never breathes the fresh air; or the baker bending into his oven[2]. We can hardly suppose that the pressure on labourers in the time of the Middle Empire was less than it had been in the usual conditions of the Old Empire.

There is however one important feature which distinguishes this period from the time of the Pyramid builders; it is obvious that Egypt was emerging from the isolation which had formerly characterised it. Tentative experiments of the kind had indeed been made under Pepy I. and his successors in the sixth dynasty[3] (B.C. 3447); but from that time onwards there is a long period during which the events of Egyptian history are wrapped in deep obscurity; and when they once more come into light, under the twelfth dynasty, it seems as if the Pharaohs had lost whatever footing their predecessors may formerly have had outside the limits of Egypt proper.

There are three sides on which Egypt might most easily be brought into communication with the outside world. On the north-west were the tribes of Libya; and it is clear from the monuments, that these peoples were frequently seen in Egypt. Occasional attacks were made from this quarter, but the resources of the desert did not attract the cupidity of the Pharaohs. The case was very different with the Sinaitic

---

[1] Their "corporations" do not appear to have been gilds of independent workers, but "gangs" of men working under a contractor on a part of a large operation. Erman, *Life*, 123. They are possibly analogous to the lodges of fourteenth century masons in England.

[2] Maspero, *Dawn*, 314.

[3] Flinders Petrie, *History*, I. 94, 99.

peninsula, which was accessible from the east of Memphis. The "lords of the sands" were so often hostile that it was important they should be kept in check and subdued; especially as the peninsula was rich in copper and in turquoise. The Pyramid builders had apparently had access to this region, and Pepy I. had succeeded in working the mines again, after his general Una had waged five great campaigns against the Bedouin and their allies [1]. Under the twelfth dynasty a regular colony was established at the mines, and forts were erected to protect the workings from the Bedouin, though no attempt was made to acquire more territory than was necessary in order to secure access to this mineral wealth [2].

Still more tempting were the products which could be obtained by pushing southwards along the valley of the Nile. Here also the conquering armies had been led by Una [3], and the negroes were so completely subdued that they were forced to serve in other Egyptian campaigns; while a successful attempt was made to navigate the first cataract with boats containing a huge block of alabaster. Under the eleventh and twelfth dynasties there were similar expeditions: so that the Egyptians obtained access to regions from which large supplies of gold could be obtained [4], and eventually so far reduced them to obedience as to be able to control the working of the Nubian mines, which are situated in the country between the first and second cataracts. Thus another source of mineral wealth was brought within the reach of Egyptian sovereigns; while each of these wars was something of a slave raid and

---

[1] Maspero, *Dawn*, 421.

[2] Maspero, *Histoire Ancienne*, 101. It seems that under the twelfth dynasty the colony communicated with Egypt by sea, not by the desert. Erman, *Life*, p. 505.

[3] *Records of Past*, II. 3.

[4] Under Usertesen I. (eleventh dynasty) the boundary of Egypt was pushed as far as the second cataract, and this point was protected by fortifications under the twelfth dynasty. Maspero, *Dawn*, 478.

resulted in the capture of large numbers of prisoners[1]. We can see that the policy deliberately pursued was that of capturing the population, and destroying the resources of the plundered country so that by making a desert they might secure immunity from attack. This is especially noticeable in campaigns against the Lords of the Sands and their allies on the north[2].

The Egyptians under the Middle Empire were steadily extending their political influence and turning it to account as a means of increasing their resources. Their land was also being brought into connection with other countries by commerce. It was not so situated that the desire for commercial intercourse could naturally arise from within; the main routes of land carriage lay outside the Nile valley on the west, and on the farther side of the Red Sea on the east. But the Pharaohs of the Middle Empire made an arrangement for tapping both streams of commerce, by providing such facilities for travelling across Egypt through Koptos that the district around Thebes was brought into direct contact with the main avenues of land commerce, and was no longer limited to the products which could be obtained by the Nile route.

There is little reason to believe that the Egyptians themselves engaged in active commerce and made use of the routes to which they now had access. We find merchants of many races, Libyan and Semitic, frequenting Egypt, but there is little reason to believe that the Egyptians themselves travelled far afield for the sake of commerce. The Sinaitic desert appears to have been a considerable thoroughfare for trade, but it was carried on by Ishmaelites, such as brought Joseph down into Egypt. Though the Egyptian reputation was high, the Egyptian influence extended but a little way north-eastwards[3],

[1] Erman, *Life,* 523.

[2] Erman, *Life,* 522. The preserving the country as a source of tribute was the policy of the New Empire in Syria.

[3] *Records of the Past,* VI. 135. The story of Sanehat in the twelfth

and Sanehat, a political suspect under the twelfth dynasty[1], had not far to go to escape the possibility of recognition and recapture; he found himself after a brief journey among the Bedouin, from whom he had an honourable reception[2]; the carrying of goods across the desert was done, not by the Egyptians, but by Semitic tribes. Indeed the narratives of the early portion of Genesis are typical illustrations of a movement which was going on rapidly at this time, of visits of Semitic merchants to Egypt, to be followed up by Semitic settlements in Egypt.

The case is somewhat different as regards intercourse by sea; the valley which leads from Koptos towards the sea furnished a rich red porphyry which was particularly admired; the work of quarrying it involved enormous labour, but it was pushed on with assiduity. In the time of the eleventh dynasty the project seems to have been carried out of forcing a road through this valley and establishing a colony near Kosseir on the coast of the Red Sea[3]. On the route thus opened up an unexpected supply of water was found[4], and the colony was made the depot from which the mining district of the Sinaitic peninsula could be reached. It also served as a port from which occasional expeditions could be organised to the land of "Punt." The earliest of those which went by this route was apparently organised by Henu[5] under the eleventh dynasty; and from that time onwards Egyptian shipping must have been frequently seen on the Red Sea as well as on the Nile. The legend of the shipwrecked sailor who was

dynasty gives an interesting account of the country to the east of the Isthmus at this time. It is also clear that Egypt was fortified against the raids from the desert.

[1] Flinders Petrie, *History*, I. 153.

[2] Compare the demand of Moses under the New Empire for a three days' journey into the Wilderness.

[3] Maspero, *Histoire Ancienne*, p. 94.

[4] Erman, *Life*, 473.

[5] *Ib.* 506.

entertained with polite conversation by a friendly snake[1] on a magic island is conclusive as to the seafaring habits of the Egyptians of the Middle Empire, so far as the Red Sea is concerned.

The mysterious land of Punt, from which such treasures were brought, was not so much a particular district, as a geographical expression for the whole of the lands from which the various products came that reached Egypt from the south by way of the Red Sea. Arabian, Persian and even Indian products would be brought in this manner: but the district which was chiefly in view was the Somali coast of Africa, on the Gulf of Aden, as incense could be procured from thence.

These maritime expeditions can hardly be regarded as really commercial. They may be thought of partly as voyages of discovery[2] and partly as embassies sent to distant potentates. The exchange of goods which took place was represented by the Egyptians as a sort of tribute, and we are apt to speak of it as commerce, but it was not exactly either one or the other. Political and commercial elements were both present, and it is not possible to say which was dominant. The transaction may be best described as one of *mutual gifts*; the amount given in such cases depends partly on the real or assumed status of the giver and receiver respectively and not merely on the marketable value of the things[3]. The story of the Queen of Sheba's visit to Jerusalem may be taken as an example of a similar expedition at a somewhat later date.

Still this intercourse with other lands reacted on the social

---

[1] Erman, *Life*, 508.

[2] Compare the anxiety of a Pharaoh of the sixth dynasty to see a dwarf, and the care taken about his health. Maspero, *Dawn*, 433. The voyages organised by Prince Henry the Navigator offer a parallel.

[3] The element of bargaining is present, but there are no competitors, either buyers or sellers, and therefore scarcely a market. On the exchange of "gifts" in Egypt (New Empire) see Maspero, *Struggle*, 280. Also in modern Persia, Browne, *Year in Persia*, p. 67.

condition of Egypt in more ways than one. The occasional campaign furnished prisoners who could be treated as slaves, and sent to work in the mines. In the time of Pepy, the Sinaitic mines had been partly worked by the forced labour of the Nile population[1], but the conquests of the Bedouin by Una furnished a supply of slaves which rendered it possible to dispense with excessive corvées[2]. At a later date, the mines of Nubia were worked entirely by slaves, and Diodorus Siculus gives a harrowing account of the severity of their labour and the wretchedness of their lives[3]. The time of warlike contact with neighbouring lands was the time when slave labour on a large scale was introduced, and could be maintained as a regular thing, though the supply of slaves was not entirely drawn from abroad, but was at all events supplemented from criminal or unfortunate Egyptians.

An effect, which was perhaps of greater importance politically, though of less interest economically, was the settlement of considerable colonies of Semites, within and on the outskirts of the Nile valley. There were fisherfolk of Phoenician type who lived on the east of the Delta and plied their art in the lagoon known as Lake Menzaleh. The story of Abraham's temporary residence in Egypt is an illustration of a movement that was beginning to show itself; and it is at least probable that the Syrian people already traded to Egypt in the Mediterranean waters and had factories in the towns of the Delta. Indeed, it would seem that the whole of the country was strongly influenced by this new element, and that a fashion for adopting Semitic phrases affected the literature of the time[4]. Just as the way was prepared for the Norman conquest

[1] Maspero, *Dawn*, 356.

[2] *Ib.* 421.

[3] Diodorus Siculus, III. 12–14. The account of the processes employed and of the division of labour is graphic.

[4] Compare Brugsch, c. xi. The influx of Semitic fashion was more striking under the New Empire.

of England by an immigration of Norman administrators and a prevalence of Norman fashions, so it may be said that the Semitic influence, which had come in peacefully, contributed to the success of the invasion by which the Middle Empire was eventually overthrown.

12.   III.   There is an interesting analogy between the struggle which destroyed the Theban Empire, about two thousand years B.C., and the incursions of barbarian hordes into the Roman Empire, many centuries later. Both began with a distinct movement of the nations, the precise reasons of which are unknown; both invasions were aided by men who had settled on the borders of the empire; and in both cases, after a bitter struggle, the machinery of government fell into the hands of the invaders. The cruelties which were perpetrated by the Shepherd Kings, in fighting their way to power in Egypt, were long remembered with horror[1]: but there is this great difference between the two invasions. The barbarians broke the power of Rome in the lands they conquered and swept it away for ever; in Egypt there was enough of patriotic spirit left among the conquered to find expression in successful vengeance. For a hundred and fifty years a war of independence was waged, and when it at length proved successful, the Pharaohs of the Theban Empire entered on a series of wars of revenge. They were inspired with a new ambition; not only—like the Memphite emperors—to perpetuate their memory for all time, but to make their power felt in distant places as well. Egypt aspired to build up an empire that should extend from the Euphrates to the confines of Ethiopia; and the wealth obtained by successful conquest was used to erect the magnificent temples which may still be seen at Luxor and Karnak. The most magnificent of the halls at the latter place was built by Sety I.[2] (B.C. 1327), the same Pharaoh who undertook another great public work during this

Luxor and Karnak.

---

[1] Maspero, *Histoire Ancienne*, 164.
[2] Brugsch, II. 10.

period, and cut a canal which connects the Bitter Lakes;
though he thus anticipated the Suez Canal for a part of its
course, his work was more probably undertaken as a frontier
defence, than for commercial reasons [1].

During this period the connection between the history of
Egypt and the familiar narratives of the Book of Genesis
becomes closer. It seems to have been under Apepa, a king
of the first Hyksos dynasty, that Joseph was sent into Egypt
and rose to power as an administrator. The war of independence was unfavourable to the fortunes of the Israelites as
of other Semites who remained in Egypt after the expulsion of
the Hyksos; they were treated as a conquered race, and were
in some cases subjected to oppression that could not be distinguished from actual slavery [2]. Though it was weakened by
other causes, the fall of this restored Egyptian empire appears
to have been in part occasioned by that revolt of the servile
Semites which we speak of as the Exodus.

So far as the relations of Egypt with the southern peoples
are concerned, there was no decided change in character during
this new period as compared with the old. So soon as the
invaders were driven out, the Pharaohs set themselves to re-
establish their empire in Nubia; the campaigns were most
successful, and their conquests were pushed from the line of
the second cataract as far south as that of the fourth; but the
expeditions continued to be mere slave raids, though on an
extended scale. So too, the great voyage to the land of Punt
which was organised under Queen Hatshepsut does not differ
in character from previous enterprises, though it seems to have
been more successful than any previous expedition. The
records which remain supply most interesting pictures of the
Egyptian ships, and of the Somali king and queen whose land
they visited [3]. Many rare products were brought back to Egypt,

[1] Erman, *Life*, 537.
[2] Maspero, *Struggle*, 88.
[3] Flinders Petrie, *History*, II. 83.

but they were obtained by an exchange of gifts rather than in the course of trade.

It was in its relations to Syria—the side from which the Hyksos had come—that the ancient policy was reversed; hitherto, the colony on the Sinaitic peninsula had been a solitary attempt at the extension of Egyptian power into Asia. The isthmus had been the immemorial frontier of Egypt; but now, when Tahutmes I. undertook a war of revenge and led a vast army across the desert and through Syria as far as the Euphrates, the Egyptians must have felt as if a new world was opened up to them. Over the large area that was thus subdued, the Pharaohs attempted to establish a sort of suzerainty, and to exact a regular tribute. They were able to exercise an effective authority over towns like Gaza in the south, but their hold on the more distant peoples was of the slightest, and Egypt was involved in not a few costly campaigns, in the effort to maintain what was at best little more than a nominal suzerainty.

The real importance of the wars of Tahutmes was that they brought the Egyptians into relations with civilizations that were comparable with and in some ways superior to their own; regular intercourse was established with peoples who were not mere barbarians, but who had a right to be treated as equals. When the empire of Tahutmes extended to the Euphrates, he was brought into contact with the Chaldeans. The alluvial soil at the mouth of the Euphrates had offered appropriate conditions for the growth of a power which was curiously similar to Egypt in its political character and intellectual life, but different in its economic products. The cereals of Chaldaea were much more varied than those of Egypt; there was a greater variety of domesticated animals. The horse and the camel had been unknown in Egypt till Semitic influence began to be felt; but during the Hyksos period, if not before, the horse had been completely acclimatised, and Tahutmes went to the fray well provided with horses and chariots. Even at

this later date Chaldaea excelled in the manufacture and dyeing of woollen goods, while Egypt's chief textile manufacture
was working up linen. The successful war opened up a route
for organised commerce, just as in later ages the Crusades
brought about a vast demand for Eastern products in Western
Europe and led to the development of trade. As Maspero
writes[1], "Whole convoys of spoil were despatched to Egypt
after every successful campaign, and their contents were distributed in varying proportions among all classes of society...
These distributions must have stimulated a passion for all
Syrian goods, and as the spoil was insufficient to satisfy the
increasing demands of the consumer, the waning commerce
which had been carried on from early times was once more
revived and extended, till every route whether by land or
water between Thebes, Memphis and the Asiatic cities was
thronged by those engaged in its pursuit." The imports into
Egypt[2] comprised not only slaves, but animals of various kinds,
horses to improve native breeds, and curiosities like bears and
elephants, or birds with brilliant plumage; building materials,
especially wood, with which Egypt was badly provided, as well
as dyed and embroidered stuffs, which were more generally
used for furniture than for dress. The trade thus developed
came to be a source of revenue, as customs were levied at the
ports and frontiers of Egypt[3]. The trade which thus sprang
up between Chaldaea and Egypt as its goals, with the intermediate countries as contributories, was very valuable and did
much to determine the course of Egyptian politics.

It appears that a desire to maintain authority over the
peoples of Syria and to secure conditions for the continuance
of this trade, first brought the Pharaohs into hostile relations
with the Hittites. They were an enterprising people, vigorous

---

[1] Maspero, *Struggle*, 283.
[2] Erman, *Life*, 516.
[3] Maspero, *Struggle*, 286. Sayce, *Patriarchal Palestine*, 84. Brugsch,
Aegyptologie, 216.

alike in trade and in war; and from their homes on Mount Taurus they exercised a wide influence both by sea and land. The support which they gave enabled the Syrian peoples to withdraw from the payment of tribute to their Egyptian lords, and at the same time to plunder the trading caravans with impunity. In order to re-establish his power and to maintain the supplies, it was necessary for Tahutmes III. to engage in several campaigns in Syria; his greatest achievements were in humbling the Hittites and obtaining possession of their city of Kadesh on the Orontes; but even his victories, magnificent though they were[1], failed to give more than a temporary check to the growing power of the Hittites; and Ramessu II., the Pharaoh of the oppression, found it wisest to make a treaty with their king, as an equal. It contains some very curious extradition clauses, especially one which seems to imply[2] that Hittite workmen were not to be tempted into settling in Egypt, and by introducing their arts into the dominions of the Pharaohs to limit the scope for trade.

The existence of such treaties goes to show that Egypt was no longer predominant in the Syrian lands, and that the glories of the New Empire were already on the wane. The Asiatic power had been built up by the conquests of Tahutmes I. and Tahutmes III., but it was very unwieldy, and the revenue which had been derived from tribute provinces was difficult to collect. The practice of making royal presents to those who brought the tribute[3] may be regarded as part of the expense of collection, but if the presents were not costly the

[1] Brugsch, I. 318.

[2] This is the interpretation put on it by Maspero, *Struggle*, 286. *Records of Past*, IV. 25; Brugsch, II. 73. In the eighteenth century A.D. there was much anxiety about the transplanting of trades by the emigration of workmen from England. It may be inferred from the text that the Pharaohs encouraged alien immigrants, but there was no cause to fear emigration to Syria.

[3] Brugsch, I. 437.

recipients were dissatisfied and the difficulties of getting any tribute in subsequent years were increased[1]. In the more distant provinces it could only be obtained when an armed force was actually present.

These political difficulties in controlling Asiatic possessions were not peculiar to this age, but were also felt by the Ptolemies and others who have tried to make the Nile valley the basis of an Asiatic empire; the physical conditions which isolated Egypt economically for so long, rendered it impossible for her to exercise a wide sway as a political power by land[2]. In the time of the New Empire, however, there were also causes of weakness within Egypt itself; for this one period in its long history Egypt ceased to be self-sufficing as regards its food supply, and had to exact corn as a tribute from other lands[3]; perhaps the labour of the Egyptian population was diverted from agriculture to other employments. It may have been that the difficulties thus created tempted Ramessu II. to put full pressure on the servile population, but they were at length goaded into an insurrection[4].

While the prosperity of the Egyptian Empire was being thus undermined, an additional strain was put on its military resources, as the country was assailed from different sides, so that there was now need to repel attacks from the tribes on the west and an insurrection in the south. The government was not strong enough to face this accumulation of disasters, and Egypt sank from a position of great military glory to a condition of general misery and decay, and subjection to foreign powers. A great part of the wealth of the Pharaohs, whether derived from tribute or trade, had been dependent on her political and military greatness, and when these were sapped, the material prosperity of the Empire was overthrown.

[1] Maspero, *Struggle*, 278.
[2] Pharaoh Neco and the Ptolemies had some commerce over the sea.
[3] Flinders Petrie, *History*, II. 149.
[4] Brugsch, II. 99.

C. W. C.

3

13   From the time when the supremacy of Egypt was thus
overthrown she never recovered her old greatness,

*Assyrian and
Ethiopian
Supremacy.*

and for several succeeding centuries she suffered
subjection alternately to her old tributaries in
Ethiopia and in the north. Her isolation was broken down f
ever : she had ceased to be a conqueror, but the traditi
her inexhaustible productivity remained, and she continu
be the prey of one military power after another. The
interest in the period of her decadence is that of try
to trace the links of connection by which the heritage of
industrial skill, which she had developed, was transported to
other parts of the world.

There were indeed seasons of revival, when Egypt flourished
once more for a time; Ramessu III. built forts to protect his
land from invasion, and devoted himself to the development of
commerce, while he was also a successful general who repelled
a great invasion and carried out an effective war of revenge.
He seems to have come in contact with the people of Caria,
Cilicia and Cyprus[1]. But even this epoch of success bears
witness to the depression and decline which had overtaken the
country, for the monuments of this period show no trace of the
artistic excellence which had characterised the productions of
more vigorous days. In the general disorder which affected
the realm, the priestly caste attained to greater and greater
dignity till at length one of them ascended the throne, as
the result of a successful revolution : but the cause of the
dispossessed line was taken up by a powerful neighbour, and
the country was conquered by the Assyrians. Sheshonk, the
son of Nimrod[2], established a new dynasty and reduced to a
subordinate position the Pharaoh of the priestly line, whose
daughter Solomon had married. At this point numerous links

---

[1] Brugsch, II. 153. The strong Semitic influence acting on Egypt at
this period is seen in the development of trade with Syria. The Greek
islands, except Cyprus and Crete, were probably unknown as yet to the
Egyptians. Erman, *Life in Ancient Egypt*, 515.   [2] Brugsch, II. 219.

connect the history of Egypt with that of Israel. Sheshonk
had been the protector of Jeroboam, and one of his most
successful expeditions was an invasion of Judah in the time of
Rehoboam. But the new invaders were even less successful
than the Hyksos in establishing a permanent rule. The
descendants of the exiled priests raised a formidable power
in Ethiopia: they first attained to independence and then
made a successful attack upon the foreign rulers of Egypt.
The ancient line had opened up the way for the establishment
of an Assyrian dynasty; the priestly line had their revenge in
time, but only with the result of establishing an Ethiopian
dynasty. Thus rebellion and invasion led eventually to dis-
memberment, and it was only at a time of Assyrian weakness
that the founder of the twenty-sixth dynasty was able to concentrate the scattered fragments once more under a single ruler,
and to make some attempt at reviving the ancient greatness.

14. IV. This was the juncture at which Pharaoh Neco
succeeded to the throne: and the short-lived
period of Egyptian prosperity, which commenced   Pharaoh
with his reign, is curiously different from any   Neco.
that had gone before. He was not satisfied with reliance on
the inherent resources of the land, its inexhaustible fertility
and mineral wealth, but he also tried to obtain command of
the sea. This ambition forced him to seek the assistance
of foreigners, and especially of the Greeks, who seem to have
been the most skilled naval architects of the time. Their
triremes were now more formidable ships than any that had
been constructed by the Phoenicians. Two fleets of triremes,
of Greek pattern probably, were built for Neco[1], one on the
Mediterranean and one on the Red Sea, and the cities of Sais
and Naucratis were full of Greek merchants and immigrants[2].

---

[1] Herodotus, II. 159.
[2] Naucratis was refounded by Amasis about 570 B.C., but it seems to
have been a centre of trade for more than a century previously. Flinders
Petrie, *Naucratis* 4. (Egypt Exploration Fund.)

The new development of Egyptian life was really due to their influence, and when the political ambition of Neco was finally destroyed by the defeat which he suffered from the Babylonians at Carchemish in 605 B.C., the commercial activity still continued.

The greatest of Neco's public works was unsuccessful: he attempted to reopen a canal which had been dug long before under Sety, and to obtain a means of uniting his two fleets. There seems to have been an extraordinary loss of life in this undertaking, and the King was at length compelled to relinquish the attempt[1]; but he was not easily foiled, and he employed Phoenician sailors to start on a voyage of discovery in the hope of finding some other passage between the two seas[2]. After an absence of three years they found their way back to Egypt, having been successful in circumnavigating Africa; but the length of the voyage rendered it an unsuitable means of effecting the naval manœuvre at which Neco had aimed. It is not uninteresting to notice, however, that while Egypt

[1] 'This man (Necos) was the first who attempted the channel leading to the Erythraean Sea, which Darius the Persian afterwards completed: the length of this is a voyage of four days, and in breadth it was so dug that two triremes could go side by side driven by oars...and in the reign of Necos there perished while digging it twelve myriads of the Egyptians. Now Necos ceased in the midst of his digging, because the utterance of an oracle impeded him, which was to the effect that he was working for the Barbarian: and the Egyptians call all men Barbarians who do not agree with them in speech.' Herodotus, II. 158 (Macaulay). For the loss of life we may compare the Suez Canal; of 250,000 men employed on one part of it some 20,000 lives were sacrificed. Erman, *Life in Ancient Egypt*, p. 475.

[2] 'He (Necos), when he had ceased digging the channel which goes through the Nile to the Arabian Gulf, sent Phoenicians with ships, bidding them sail and come back through the Pillars of Hercules to the Northern Sea and so to Egypt. The Phoenicians therefore set forth from the Erythraean Sea and sailed through the Southern Sea...in the third year they turned through the Pillars of Hercules and arrived again in Egypt. And they reported a thing which I cannot believe, but another man may, namely, that in sailing round Libya they had the sun on their right hand.' Herodotus, IV. 42 (Macaulay).

developed tillage and the industrial arts with such success during the earlier periods of her greatness, it was under the auspices of an Egyptian monarch that the greatest of all the voyages of ancient times was undertaken.

In this last period then Egypt had come completely out of her isolation; she was no longer a leader in the path of economic progress, she was showing herself willing to imitate the Phoenicians and the Greeks, whose successes superseded her ancient glories. But even during this last period monuments were raised by the Egyptians which have excited the interest of subsequent ages. The gallery of the Serapeum dates from this renascence period. The prosperity of Egypt had been temporarily revived, through the imitation and with the help of alien races.

15. Egyptian history presents not a few interesting contrasts to the story of other early peoples which have contributed to Western Civilization. Alone among them she formed a great land empire; for it was only tentatively, and largely through foreign instrumentality, that she had recourse to the sea. But it is the sea that gives the means of rapid communication; it not only supplies the best means of commercial intercourse, but sea-power gives the surest assistance towards maintaining political control over distant places. Phoenicia and Greece launched forth in naval expeditions, Rome vanquished Carthage by her command of the sea, even though she laid so much stress on communications by land. The new Rome at Constantinople owed her superiority over the old Rome largely to her better maritime position; and in modern European history the importance of sovereignty at sea has been abundantly illustrated. But Egypt never attained to great power by sea: and her military empire was attained by expeditions on land.

Political Decadence, and Industrial Influence.

Hence there was never any real expansion of Egypt outside the valley of the Nile. Other peoples might be laid under contribution, and slave settlements might be formed for mining purposes : the area of Egyptian influence in the Nile valley was extended, but there were no distant colonies[1], and Egyptian civilization was not planted in other lands.   Yet Egypt was ready to draw to herself the products of other countries and the skill of other races ; she was eminently receptive, and crowds of foreigners were domiciled under her sway at different epochs.   They may often have learned from her more than they brought to her, and the practical wisdom of the Egyptians was conveyed in all directions, not by the Egyptians themselves, but by those who frequented their cities and learned their arts.

In the history of subsequent civilizations we shall have to notice how closely economic and political conditions have been connected, and how much they have reacted on one another ; but in the case of Egypt, with the exception of the last period, this interaction can scarcely be traced, because industrial and political life had hardly become distinct.   We cannot show how one thing acts on another unless the two are separate; and in ancient Egypt political power directly dominated economic life.   The great works, which move our admiration, were accomplished by slave labour or free labour ; the organisation of industry was a form of prison discipline or a method of taxation ; it cannot then be dealt with apart from the administration of the state.   In much the same way it seems that the foreign imports of Egypt were brought, not in the way of commerce for exchange, but rather as tribute from dependencies.   It was not so much the case that political power protected the interchange of goods, as that political or military pressure brought it into being.   Importation was the result of war, and in the Egyptian times the reciprocal effects of war on commerce and commerce on war do not come into sight.

In all these ways Egyptian civilization differed greatly from

---

[1] Unless the mining colony in Sinai be classed as such.

that of the various races which came to the front in after
times; but its long continuance and great magnificence ought
to impress on our minds two facts which are really fundamental.
The greatness of Egypt was founded on the extraordinary rich-
ness of its products—the fertility of its soil, and the mineral
wealth it commanded. This is the most stable basis of national
prosperity; it has been the foundation on which in different
forms in different centuries the wealth of England has been
reared. But on the other hand, whatever the natural resources
of a country may be, unless there be political security and
political power to direct energy, or to maintain favourable
conditions for the display of energy by others, vast natural
resources may be wasted; they give an opportunity for, but
they cannot produce or maintain, a high and cultured civilization.

CHAPTER II.

JUDAEA.

16. THE civilization of the Israelites, even at the time of Judaea under Solomon. its greatest importance, occupies such a small place as compared with that of other great nations of antiquity, that it hardly seems to require separate treatment. It was in many ways closely dependent upon Egypt, while the most important works were carried out with the help of Phoenicians; but yet, there are good reasons for giving at least a passing glance to the history of this people. Hebraism, like Hellenism, has been an all-important factor in the development of Western Civilization; Judaism, as the precursor of Christianity, has indirectly had much to do with shaping the ideals and the morality of Western nations since the Christian era; Palestine, as a Holy Land to which Western nations looked with reverence and enthusiasm, has exercised no mean influence on the development and destinies of the West.

There is another reason which renders the recognition of this country imperative; in all subsequent ages the Jews have preserved well-marked characteristics, and in an especial manner have devoted themselves to trade and financial administration. Their special skill and success have been perpetuated from generation to generation, and in one country

after another they have been objects of jealousy to large parts
of the populations among whom they have dwelt. Under the
circumstances, we cannot but turn with interest to examine the
features of the country in which this race was nurtured, and
the special conditions of the times at which they attained their
highest prosperity.

There is no difficulty in applying our method of discrimination, and fixing on the period of the greatest material prosperity in Judaea. The Temple of Solomon was the one great
building round which the enthusiasm of the race centred; to
the raising of that temple the treasures, which David had
obtained by conquest, were devoted; and the restoration of
the fabric from its desolation was the chief hope of the pious
Jews at the time of the Captivity. There was no other public
building on which so much wealth was lavished, so much
patriotic admiration bestowed. Though, as a mere structure,
and apart from the associations which cluster round it, it was
far inferior to the Egyptian public works, it yet possesses
considerable interest. It is not easy to see how the immense
blocks which composed its foundations were brought together
and placed in position; an immense amount of labour must
have been involved in transporting the materials required for
its construction.

17. There is a marked contrast between the stories of
the empires of Solomon and of the Pharaohs.   Contrast
The latter had, in all probability, been slowly   with Egypt.
built up for centuries before the earliest of the monuments
were constructed; the former came suddenly into prominence. It is not easy for us to realise the extraordinary
rapidity of the rise of the Israelite power under Saul and
David. At the beginning of the reign of the first king, the
Israelites were in complete subjugation to the Philistines, a
tribe that had in all probability migrated from Cyprus into
Canaan not long before. They were a fishing or trading
people, who made frequent raids into the adjoining territory

and had taken good care that they should meet with little
resistance. "There was no smith found throughout all the
land of Israel; for the Philistines said, Lest the Hebrews make
them swords or spears ; but all the Israelites went down to the
Philistines to sharpen every man his share, and his coulter,
and his axe and his mattock[1]." "The people did hide themselves in caves and in thickets and in rocks and in holds and
in pits[2]." When Saul tried to organise resistance he found
that many of the people had fled beyond Jordan, and the rest
"followed him trembling[3]." The Philistines were strongly
posted in the heart of the country and "the spoilers came out
of their camps in their companies[4]." It is difficult to conceive
of any people in a more miserable plight, but there was a
sudden revolt under Saul, like that of the English tribes in the
time of Alfred. Though he was eventually killed in a last
unsuccessful contest with the Philistines at Mount Gilboa, he
had in the earlier part of his reign, organised an army[5], and
had not only thrown off the Philistine yoke, but had engaged
in offensive operations against the Ammonites, Moabites,
Edomites and Amalekites on the southern frontiers, as well as
against Zobah in the north-east. David carried on the wars
with still greater success; he humbled the Philistines utterly,
rendered the Moabites and the Syrians tributaries, and set
garrisons in Damascus as well as among the people of Edom[6].
From the river of Egypt to beyond Damascus, and southward
as far as Elath on the Red Sea[7], David established a military
empire, similar in type to the new Egyptian Empire, though
on a much smaller scale. He was able to hoard masses of
spoil and also to lay the conquered peoples under annual
contributions.

Solomon was not perfectly successful in retaining his hold

[1] 1 Sam. xiii. 19, 20.   [2] 1 Sam. xiii. 6.
[3] *Ib.* 7.   [4] *Ib.* 17.
[5] 1 Sam. xiv. 52.   [6] 2 Sam. viii. 6, 14.
[7] Maspero, *Histoire Ancienne*, 329.

on all the frontier peoples either in the south [1] or the north [2];
but on the whole he more than maintained his father's prestige.
The Egyptians had taken the Canaanitish town of Gezer, and
Solomon received it as the dower of the Egyptian princess
when he married [3]. He was able to exact tribute from all the
lands between the Euphrates and Orontes on the north, and
the river of Egypt and the gulf of Akaba on the south [4]. It
was a large tract of country and it must have furnished a considerable revenue. In its main features his empire was not
unlike that of the Pharaohs of the eighteenth dynasty, though
much smaller in area.

There is, however, a much more important point of contrast to which allusion has already been made; the civilization
of Egypt was, so far as we know, indigenous; there was, during
long periods of her history, no country ahead of her in the arts
of life, or from which she could borrow; but the people of
Israel were in close contact with two successful neighbours and
drew upon both of them. To the best of our knowledge there
is no new development of industrial art, no new departure in
commercial enterprise, that can be ascribed to the Israelites
of old; their civilization arose when they transplanted the
methods of organising labour which had been developed on
Egyptian soil [5]; but they were also deeply affected by contact
with the Phoenicians, and depended on them for industrial
skill. It was through a connection with Egypt, and contact
with Egyptian arts, that the kingdom of Solomon attained to
such a degree of splendour in so brief a time; again, this very
connection with Egypt was one of the influences which
brought about its disruption and prevented its recovery. From
the time when the Assyrians obtained a footing in Egypt the
kings of Jerusalem found frequent difficulty in even maintaining

[1] 1 Kings xi. 14, 22.   [2] *Ib.* 25.
[3] Maspero, *Histoire Ancienne*, 333.
[4] 1 Kings iv. 21.
[5] See above, § 10, p. 17.

their independence. The kingdom of Judah might have proved a useful buffer state in guarding the Egyptian frontier; but the Pharaohs were unable to support it adequately, while Judah suffered severely by being dragged again and again into the quarrels which arose between its powerful neighbours.

There is a still more striking contrast to be considered. The prosperity of Egypt under the Old and Middle Empire was maintained independently of trade; the products of the country itself furnished all the necessary materials for a vast development of wealth. The land of Israel too was fertile and well supplied with products of many kinds; but native industries had been little developed at the time of Solomon, and Israel was dependent on its neighbours for skilled labour. Much of the material as well as the skilled workmen employed on the Temple were imported, and it would hardly have been possible to draw so largely on foreign aid unless Solomon's empire had been so admirably suited for purposes of trade. The Egyptians dwelt apart from the great routes of commerce, within the natural barriers of the Nile valley; but the Israelites were, from their position, able to tap the stream of commerce between east and west.

18. Amid all the changes which have occurred in commercial history, there is wonderfully little altera-

Physical character-istics.

tion in the routes of trade. Given two districts, which are fitted by differences of character or climate to supply one another's requirements, the best means of traversing the distance between them is likely to be defined by physical conditions. This is obviously the case with river transit; and even the best course between one port and another is often prescribed by the set of ocean currents or by prevailing winds. The route which traders are compelled to take overland may be marked by the possibility of passing over mountain ranges or crossing rivers; but it is most precisely laid down in the case of caravans crossing a desert, since they are forced to make for the points where water can

be obtained. Hence it comes about that while empires and
races pass away, the old course of trade remains unchanged;
this is very noticeable in regard to the African routes across
the Sahara and Libyan deserts, but it has its bearing on the
story of Israel as well.

The territory which was claimed for Israel, and which
came under Solomon's rule, was intersected by several important trade-routes[1], while the sea-coast offered facilities for
commerce of which some of the tribes may possibly have
taken advantage as early as the time of the Judges[2]. The
commerce by land, however, was much more important;
much of it came from Petra, a town about 50 Roman miles
south of the Dead Sea; this was a very important commercial
depot, at which several caravan routes met; and from it they
divided again in various directions. One came from south-
west Arabia almost parallel with the line of the Red Sea
coast, and brought the products of Arabia Felix and of
Ethiopia. There was another route which struck right across
the desert in a westerly direction from the Persian Gulf, and
along this Oriental products were conveyed to Petra. From
Petra one road ran along the line of the Jordan through
Gilead, northwards to Damascus; another ran westwards to
Gaza, with an important branch towards Jerusalem: the third
road, which struck westwards towards Egypt, hardly concerns
us here, as it lay outside the ordinary limits of the land of
Israel; the other two, however, passed right through it.

When Solomon extended the sphere of his influence in
the north, he obtained possession of Tiphsah (Thapsacus) as
a port on the Euphrates. The caravan route thence may have
run southwards to Tadmor[3], which would form a depot similar

---

[1] Herzfeld, *Handelsgeschichte der Juden des Alterthums*, p. 22; Götz,
Verkehrswege, 92.

[2] Judges v. 17.

[3] There seems to be ground for doubting whether Tadmor was really
an ancient city; possibly the caravan route ran up the Euphrates valley,

to Petra on the south.   From Tadmor (or Damascus) one road
diverged westwards to Tyre ; and another, after crossing the
upper Jordan, led through Jezreel to the country of the Philistines and to Egypt.   Thus the great stream of commerce
between the Euphrates valley and Egypt passed right through
the land of Israel from north-east to south-west ; while those
from Arabia and Petra to Damascus and Tyre, traversed the
country from south to north.   Caravans of merchants passing
along these routes were familiar sights even in the early days
when Joseph's brethren sold him into Egyptian slavery.

The land of Israel was fertile and well provided with the
supplies which these caravans would require ; and it profited
by the trade which was transmitted along the highways of the
commerce of the known world.   Egypt had been, as we have
seen, practically precluded from commerce by its position ;
the people of Israel, on the other hand, had settled in a
land where they could not avoid it if they would.   The Old
Testament dilates in familiar passages on the physical advantages of Palestine for tillage and vineyards ; but it does
not bring out to the ordinary reader the unique facilities
which the Israelites enjoyed for engaging in trade.   It was
in this respect that they were at a marked advantage when
compared with the land of Egypt.

19.   The extraordinary facilities which were thus afforded
Caravan   become clear when we remember the special cha-
trade.   racteristics of intercommunication conducted by
caravans.   A railway may pass through a country, and have
but little effect upon it ; modern trade may go through it
without touching it at all, or giving it much opportunity of
gaining from the transit.   But the caravan must halt from
time to time for rest and refreshment, and each stopping-
place becomes a possible market.   The inhabitants of the

and thence down southwards into Palestine, not crossing the desert as
hitherto supposed.   The Tadmor of Scripture is perhaps identical with
Tamar in the wilderness of Judah.   Cf. Meyer, *Gesch. des Alt.*, I. 222, 223.

neighbouring villages may be able to sell provisions, and even water, while they have a far better opportunity of buying foreign goods, or of selling to a distant market, than peasants elsewhere. A caravan not only serves to convey goods great distances, it is also a moving market or fair which is opened at successive stages.

Such is the effect along the route; at the more important depots of trade the whole population becomes directly or indirectly connected with commerce, and the inhabitants earn a living as brokers, exchangers, or intermediaries. The process of bargaining, as conducted on such occasions, is long and tedious, and seems to require the intervention of many parties. The description of caravan trade, as Burckhardt saw it at Berber and Shendy[1], makes us feel that the inhabitants of a country so intersected as Palestine was with caravan routes, would have constant opportunities for traffic, even though they did not personally undertake such enterprises themselves.

There are some incidental allusions in the Old Testament which tend to show that there was a wide diffusion of the commercial spirit among the Israelites of old; they may be regarded as in advance of most of the neighbouring nations in this respect. The peasantry were apparently habituated to the use of money, at the time of the return from the Captivity, though we must beware of ante-dating its general introduction into ordinary transactions even in Judaea[2]. We learn from the book of Nehemiah that the landowners required money to pay their shares of the tribute[3], and we find allusions to difficulties which are closely parallel to those that occurred both in Greece and Rome, when money payments came into

---

[1] *Nubia*, I. 215, 266.   Compare also Herzfeld, *op. cit.* 23.

[2] The Parable of the Unjust Steward appears to imply the continued existence of a natural economy.

[3] Neh. v. 4.   The taxation of the Persian Empire was reorganised by Darius Hystaspis; Syria paid in money, but Egypt paid partly in corn. *Herod.* III. 91.

vogue instead of payments in kind. This change had not
been completely carried out in Nehemiah's time[1], but the
prohibitions against usury[2] seem to show that this economic
revolution had begun before the time of the Captivity. It
seems improbable, however, that the peasantry were habituated
to the use of money in ordinary life during Solomon's reign;
for it appears probable that the taxation of the country was
levied in commodities and service[3]. Solomon had twelve
officers who provided victuals for the king and his household,
each man having to make provision for a month in the year.
They may have been purveyors who purchased the necessary
supplies, but it seems more likely that the supply of food was
levied as a tax payable in kind[4]. Food was undoubtedly
required; and a levy of this sort might be the easiest way
of securing it, but so long as the expensive and inconvenient
method of collecting revenue in kind continues to be in vogue
in any land, it is improbable that money will have come into
common use for other purposes; while it seems probable that
some of the tribute of conquered peoples was also paid in
kind[5]. But, though this served for internal taxation, there
can be little doubt that Solomon would exact a revenue in
money or gifts from the trader who passed along the caravan
route which traversed the country. There was abundant opportunity for levying tolls; this is the most obvious way of raising
a revenue, and may have been the underlying cause of many of
the disputes of which we read in the Old Testament history[6].

---

[1] Neh. v. 10.

[2] Exodus xxii. 25; Lev. xxv. 36, 37; Deut. xxiii. 19, 20.

[3] 1 Kings iv. 7.

[4] 1 Kings iv. 6, 7 and 22—24. Compare the Domesday phrase, *firma
unius noctis*.

[5] Mesha, king of Moab, paid 100,000 rams and 100,000 lambs as tribute
to Ahab: he probably paid in the same fashion earlier. 2 Kings iii. 4.

[6] The conflict of the Philistines and Israel at Gilboa has been attributed
to a desire to push the Hebrew influence along the great caravan road.
Maspero, *Histoire Ancienne*, 324.

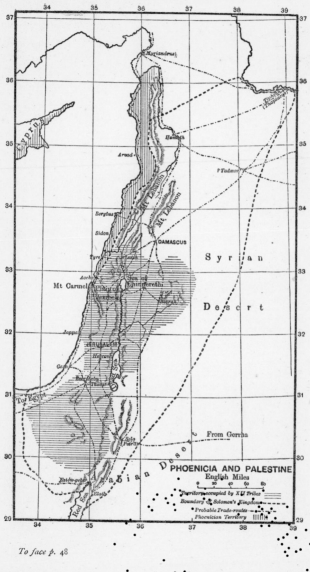

PHOENICIA AND PALESTINE
English Miles

Territory occupied by XII Tribes
Boundary of Solomon's Kingdom
Probable Trade-routes
Phoenician Territory

S.Myriandrus

?Thapsacus

Hamath

CYPRUS

Arvad

?Tadmor

Mt. Lebanon

Berytus

Sidon

Mt. Lebanon

Tyre   *Maiuh*

DAMASCUS

S y r i a n

Acchu   Sea of
Chinnereth

Mt Carmel *Dimon*
Hesbon

Bozrah

D e s e r t

Joppa

JERUSALEM

Hebron

Gaza

Beersheba
Tamar

To Egypt

From Gerrha

*Sela
Petra*

A r a b i a n   D e s e r t

Ezion-geber

Elath

Red Sea

20. There can at least be no doubt that Solomon, as
King of Judah and Israel, took full advantage   Royal Com-
of his position in order to engage in trade on   merce.
his own account. He founded commercial emporia at convenient points, and organised expeditions which were similar to
the Egyptian voyages to the land of Punt. "The king had
at sea a navy of Tarshish with the navy of Hiram; once every
three years came the navy of Tarshish, bringing gold, and
silver, ivory, and apes, and peacocks[1]." It is worth noticing
too that the Israelites were dependent on Phoenician assistance, not only for Mediterranean voyages as the Egyptians
had been, but for the expeditions on the Red Sea as well.
Solomon "made a navy of ships in Ezion-geber[2]," on the
shore of the Red Sea. "And Hiram sent in the navy his
servants, shipmen that had knowledge of the sea, with the
servants of Solomon. And they came to Ophir, and fetched
from thence gold, four hundred and twenty talents, and
brought it to king Solomon." We may perhaps gather that
the men of Israel were not apt pupils; for on the occasion
when we read of another attempt of the same kind it proved
a disastrous failure[3]; and Jehoshaphat does not seem to have
thought that the servants of Ahaziah would be a real assistance in his undertaking. It seems to be even more true of
Israel than of the people of Egypt—at least in the New
Empire—that they showed no aptitude for maritime enterprise.

There is more interest about royal trading by land; for
this, so far as we know, was not directly borrowed from the
Egyptians. King Solomon appears to have organised a commercial department of state, and to have conducted a large
trade between Egypt and the kings of Syria and the Hittites.
Horses had become naturalised in the Nile valley under Semitic
influence; and the Egyptian breed was specially valued for

[1] 1 Kings x. 22.   [2] 1 Kings ix. 26—28.
[3] 1 Kings xxii. 48.

C. W. C.   4

chariots of war. Linen yarn too was another article of royal trading[1], and Solomon seems to have done a large business at regulated prices, which were doubtless calculated so as to leave a handsome profit. The organisation of commercial enterprise as a department of Government administration is not unfamiliar in later history—in the Venetian fleets or the Dutch East Indian Companies, in much of the organisation of French commerce, and even in the finance of Edward III; but it is not clear that the later kings, either of Judah or Israel, continued to conduct such business, or that their subjects engaged in foreign trade. In a moment of humiliation Ben-hadad offered Ahab trading privileges in Damascus[2]; but there is no proof that any advantage was taken of this proposal. Still, the tradition of the commerce of Solomon's time survived to supply colour to the prophetic visions. Isaiah's picture of Jerusalem—frequented by caravans of Midianites, with the gold of Sheba and the wool of Kedar, supplied with wealth by the ships of Tarshish and the products of Lebanon, and served by the sons of strangers—is a reflection of the conditions which held good for a time under Solomon; though the prophet could not forget the darker features of the story and the cause of the fall of the earlier empire. " I will also make thy officers peace, and thine exactors righteousness[3]." How far this imported wealth in the actual monarchy was due to trade, and how far it was of the nature of tribute from dependent states, we have hardly sufficient data to determine. The transactions between Hiram and Solomon are perhaps best described as mutual gifts[4]; it is not easy to say how far they had a commercial and how far they had a political character.

21. The natural productiveness of the country, coupled with the facilities for trade, must have militated seriously against the development of industry.

Conditions of Industry.

---

[1] 1 Kings x. 28, 29. [2] 1 Kings xx. 34. [3] Isaiah lx. 17.
[4] 1 Kings v. 8—11; Is. lx. 11—14. See above, p. 26.

When the productions of Egypt, Chaldea and Phoenicia were all readily available, there was little need to develop native manufactures; and at the time of their greatest prosperity, the people of Israel had apparently made no progress in industrial skill. The whole of the skilled work in connection with the building of the Temple appears to have been done by foreign artisans; and so far as we can judge from the incidental notices of their exports and imports in later days, there was no single manufacture in which they attained to eminence. The people of Israel appear to have directed their energies to the raising of raw products, such as wool, corn, fruit, oil, and wine, for export, while all sorts of woven and other manufactured goods were imported from abroad[1].

While they were thus under little inducement to develop native manufactures, the people of Israel appear to have been relieved from the necessity of personally undertaking the more arduous forms of drudgery. The Israelites had entered the country as conquerors, and a considerable proportion of the old population survived in a state of servitude—like that of the Semites in Egypt during the New Empire. On them Solomon levied forced labour, but he did not make bondmen of the children of Israel; they only served him in administrative capacities[2]. There was a huge body of labourers employed in obtaining materials at Lebanon; and thirty thousand, presumably of the subject peoples in the land of Israel[3], had to spend one month out of three in forced labour in the quarries of Lebanon. Hence the circumstances of this halcyon period favoured the growth of a certain contempt for those who undertake the drudgery of laborious manual labour. This is implied in Isaiah's description of the new kingdom, where arduous labour should fall to the lot of the Gentiles, but it also finds expression in the

---

[1] Herzfeld, *Handelsgeschichte der Juden*, 118.

[2] 1 Kings ix. 20—22.   [3] 1 Kings v. 13.

4—2

passage in *Ecclesiasticus*[1] where the life of cultured leisure is contrasted with that of manual toil. Though it is by no means an exclusively Jewish habit of thought, this dislike for industrial occupations has been commonly regarded in later ages as a characteristic feature of the Jewish race.

22. The division of King Solomon's empire into two kingdoms, neither of which was strong enough to exercise a wide influence, rendered the Israelites more dependent than before on their powerful neighbours; and after an unequal struggle, both one realm and the other were completely absorbed by the Assyrians. It is interesting to notice, however, that this fatal severance was directly due to the heavy exactions which had been imposed in Solomon's time; the exactions of food from the Israelites and of forced labour from the subject-population had been felt to be an intolerable burden. When Rehoboam refused to diminish the heavy exactions of his father, ten tribes revolted against him[2]. The heavy taxation within the land brought about revolt and loss of prestige; with the loss of prestige, the power of exacting revenue from neighbouring states must have been seriously diminished. The break-up and decline of Solomon's empire can thus be distinctly traced to economic causes.

The Apti-
tudes of the
Race.

Still this empire, short-lived though it was, has left a deep mark on subsequent civilization; not by contributing any special art or definite type of organisation, but by forming a race which, in its dispersion, has perpetuated and preserved the habits and character formed in Palestine under the rule of Solomon. About the aptitude of the Jews there can be no doubt, whether we praise it as business ability or blame it by some harsher name. They have not devoted themselves to industrial employment nor shown the enterprise which opens new markets or pushes fresh lines of discovery,

[1] Ecclesiasticus xxxviii. 3², 33.
[2] 1 Kings xii. 14.

but they have patiently pursued the humbler courses of commercial activity, as retailers and brokers, while they have at times attained wealth and position by the skill with which they have discharged administrative functions, and shewed themselves faithful servants of government. The fields of activity to which they have betaken themselves, as aliens in after ages, are just those which were open and attracted them when Solomon reigned in all his glory.

CHAPTER III.

THE PHOENICIANS.

23. To the historian of commerce the Phoenicians are
more interesting than any other nation of
antiquity; but yet there is no people in regard
to whom our information is more meagre. The
monuments which they raised in Phoenicia have
been destroyed, not only by the ravages of time, but by the
destructive activity of man[1], while there are no records or
works of native historians to which we can turn. It may be
said that almost all we know of them comes from incidental
allusions in the records of other peoples; and as the commercial activity of the Phoenicians brought them into contact
with many other lands, we are able to piece together some
fragments of authentic history. Thus we learn from Egyptian
sources that there was a Tyrian quarter in Memphis as early
as 1250 B.C.; Hebrew literature gives us some information
regarding that Hiram who refounded Tyre (1028 B.C.); from
his time its greatness may be dated. In the Old Testament
we also read of a later king of Tyre, Ith-baal, the father of
Jezebel. It was in connection with the troubles that disturbed
the dynasty he established that the colony of Carthage was

*Settlement
in Phoenicia
and Physical
Conditions.*

---

[1] Renan, *Mission de Phénicie*, 817.

refounded[1], and that the independent[2] influence of Tyre began to decline. It is not from any words of their own, but by incidental reference in the histories of other nations that the principal dates in Phoenician history can be fixed.

Herodotus has preserved for us the Persian traditions about the origin of this people; it was said that they had migrated from the Persian Gulf to the shores of the Mediterranean[3]. The founders of the older Tyre and Sidon may be looked upon as establishing a group of fishing and commercial colonies, precisely similar to those which emanated from Phoenicia at a later date. The Persian Gulf was the scene of fishing industries and maritime trade from early times, and the Phoenician colonists may be regarded as the advanced guard of that Semitic invasion of Syrian lands, which culminated in the successful campaigns of the Hyksos and the conquest of Egypt.

The few surviving indications, as to the character of the Phoenician cities, seem to confirm this account of their origin. We probably make no serious blunder in figuring their primitive constitution to ourselves as like that of one of their own colonies. These consisted of some citizen families ruled over by judges, and maintained by the labour of a mixed multitude of a more or less servile character[4]. The colony was a fully organised community before it started for its new home; when we consider how ready Oriental monarchs were to deport entire populations, we cannot regard the migration of such a commercial community from the Persian Gulf to the coast of Syria as at all unlikely. The towns which arose along the

[1] Carthage was founded before 1200, but rose into importance after the second foundation by Elissa in 814. Movers, *Phönizier*, II. ii. 137.

[2] On the reaction of Greek influence on Tyre and its later prosperity it is not necessary to speak here.

[3] Herodotus, I. 1.

[4] Movers, *Phönizier*, II. i. 516. In the earlier time there was probably a subject population ; in the later, trade afforded the means of purchasing numbers of slaves.

Phoenician coast were mutually independent; but they were
united in a loose confederation, which may have served for
protection against piracy, and for the settlement of fishing
disputes[1], but was not sufficiently compact to supply adequate
defence against a powerful foe.

The traditions as to the public works at Tyre confirm the
opinion which is here put forth as to the probable origin of
these cities. The great Oriental cities were for the most part
palace-cities, where the royal residence was the centre of the
whole, and the bazaars of the traders clustered near the royal
residence.   But Sidon and Tyre were from the first trading-
cities; we hear of Hiram building great harbours at Tyre, and
laying out a piazza for the merchants[2]; the temples too were
magnificent, but the royal residence does not appear to have
been particularly prominent.   Kingship was not itself primitive,
but seems to have superseded the rule of judges among the
Phoenicians, much as it did among the Israelites in the time
of Saul[3].   The cities were fundamentally commercial, in their
origin as well as in their character and constitution.

The region, on which the Phoenician immigrants had fixed
as their new home, was admirably suited for their requirements, if, as is likely enough, they had already developed
some aptitude for fishing and for trading.   When settled on
the coast of Syria, they had a considerable amount of protection
from their powerful neighbours and were thus able to pursue
their peaceful callings in comparative security; the ranges of
Lebanon were an insuperable barrier against any invader from
the East, and the spurs which go down to the coast served to
give additional safeguards.   Judaea was crushed between the

---

[1] As noted above (p. 45) the people of Dan and Asher followed maritime
employments to some extent in the time of the Judges.

[2] Rawlinson, *Phoenicia*, 42.

[3] Movers, *Phönizier*, II. i. 319.   The constitution of the Philistine cities
was probably similar: there is at least an analogy in the groups of Danish
towns in England.

rival powers of Assyria and Egypt; but Phoenicia lay in comparative safety on one side of the great plain of Esdraelon, where conclusions were so often tried. Its inhabitants fully appreciated the advantage of this comparative immunity from attack; and in the time of Hiram the Sidonians tried to secure a still stronger position by sending a large colony to reoccupy Tyre. This island city seems to have been the first of the mercantile communities which found safety, as Venice did, in the water from which she drew her wealth. In choosing the sites of their colonies abroad, the Phoenicians were careful to select positions that afforded some features of the security they enjoyed in their native country[1].

The narrow strip of land[2], on which they settled, is exceedingly fertile; it grows great quantities of corn, and the slopes which rise towards Lebanon are excellently adapted for orchards and vineyards. Their towns had an ample supply of provisions within easy range, and from an early time they were able to obtain additional corn by trade from the land of Israel. But their celebrity depends far less on the products of the soil than on the harvest of the sea. The eastern Mediterranean abounded in excellent fish, and Sidon (like Bethsaida) takes its very name from its character as a fishing haven; the coast, though rock-bound, is broken and offers many good natural harbours, some of which were improved by works, as difficult as they were magnificent. The most valuable of the resources, however, was the Tyrian *murex*, a small shell-fish which yields a tiny drop of a creamy fluid much prized as a dye. The possession of this particular commodity led the Phoenicians to devote their energies to the textile arts. In later times great quantities of wool and yarn were imported, to be woven in Tyrian looms and dressed and dyed by Tyrian craftsmen.

There were other industrial arts for which they had great

[1] As for example Gades. Kenrick, *Phoenicia*, 126.
[2] It was about 200 miles long and 35 broad at its greatest width. Rawlinson, *Phoenicia*, 2.

advantages; the hills yielded copper ore, and the Phoenicians soon became skilled in mining and in the working of metals, while they had from Lebanon a plentiful supply of timber of every kind for shipbuilding. They found ready to hand on their shores the materials which were necessary for glass-blowing; and though this was not, as Pliny[1] supposed, a native invention, it was carried to great perfection in the neighbourhood of Sidon. In this, as in most of their other industrial arts, they borrowed first from the Egyptians and later from the Greeks; but there were three exceptions; neither in woollen weaving and dyeing, nor in brass working, had they been anticipated by the people of the Nile valley[2]; and they soon excelled them in shipbuilding.

While these industrial resources lay within their reach, they had also great opportunities for commerce. The route from the Persian Gulf, which the Phoenician immigrants had traversed, as well as the caravan roads to Southern Arabia, gave them the chance of obtaining foreign products by land, while there was everything to encourage them to engage in commerce by sea. They lay within sight of Cyprus[3], and thence they were gradually led on to explore the Mediterranean from point to point, without ever venturing on an apparently aimless voyage into the open sea.

24. The most flourishing period of the commerce of the Phoenicians may be placed between the estab-
Political Weakness. lishing of the new colony at Tyre under Hiram (1028 B.C.), and the internal troubles which resulted in the foundation of Carthage (814 B.C.); during this era

----

[1] Pliny, *Nat. Hist.* XXXVI. (26), 65. Erman, *Life in Ancient Egypt*, 458.

[2] See above, § 12, p. 31.

[3] Cyprus became a particularly valuable possession to them. Its connection with the early development of copper is evidenced by the name of the metal: it had excellent forests of cedar—taller even than those of Lebanon and Taurus—and of pine. Richter, *Handel und Verkehr*, p. 4.

the fortunes of Tyre were closely connected with those of the
kingdoms of Judah and Israel. But partly perhaps from the
bent of national character and partly from their circumstances,
the Phoenician cities never attained to political greatness.
Their prosperity had been fostered by the growth of the
Egyptian Empire, and they were apparently content to live
under its shadow, so long as they could push their commercial
interests. On the whole, their adherence to Egypt served its
purpose; they had much to gain by trade with Egypt, and they
seemed to have little to fear from the great monarchies of the
East. But wealth by itself, divorced from political organisation,
may be a source of weakness rather than strength ; it may
tempt the cupidity of foreign invaders. Neither by land nor sea
were the Phoenicians really strong. There never was a common bond which brought the different cities under one rule ;
and even common dangers did not induce them to do more
than conform to a very loose federation. When they were
attacked by the Assyrians and Persians, each city was forced
to exert its energies in self-defence ; and when the weakest
had fallen, its ships were available for the subjugation of the
rest. Phoenicia could never vie with the great land empires
of Egypt and Assyria, nor did it retain such a hold upon its
colonies as to form a maritime power that could concentrate
its forces at valuable points and repel attack. Phoenicia had
no political unity, and despite its wealth, had very little power.
Tyre, with all its wealth, succumbed alike to Nebuchadnezzar
(574 B.C.) and to Alexander (332 B.C.).

At the same time it may be noticed that the type of
organisation, which was then developed, was admirably fitted
for its purpose ; and something very similar has arisen at
different epochs in later times. Greek colonisation may be
regarded as a direct imitation of that of the Phoenicians ;
but the inter-municipal commerce, which sprang up in the
twelfth and thirteenth centuries after Christ, was practically an
independent growth. The towns of mediæval Christendom

differed very much from one another in origin and history;
and yet as commercial centres, with frequent inter-communi-
cation, they offer interesting analogies to the colonies and
factories which were planted by the Phoenicians on the shores
and islands of the Mediterranean. They had little political
life, but they developed a wide-spread system of inter-municipal
commerce.

25. We have not sufficient data to follow the course of
colonisation with any precision; but there can be
little doubt that trade would precede attempts
at settlement, and that, when any products were
offered which were specially valued by the Phoenicians, they
would be anxious to obtain access to the sources of supply.
They were attracted by anything that supplemented their own
resources at home, especially by opportunities of fishing either
for the tunny or the murex, and of mining for precious or
useful metals. It seems likely that they also took account
of the supply of naval stores, while it is highly probable that
they also had depots from which they procured wool and slaves.
In Egypt their commercial settlements were mere factories, as
the Pharaohs would not allow them any independence; but in
other countries each community had practical autonomy, and
complete control over the material resources within its reach.

The period of Sidonian colonisation may be said to have
closed with the building of Tyre; but before this date the
Phoenicians had already gone far afield. They probably first
found their way to Cyprus, attracted by the rich veins of copper,
as well as by the silver and iron which that island affords[1].
There they founded Paphos and other cities, both on the south
coast and in the interior; they probably worked their way westwards along the coast of Asia Minor; and certain traces[2] of
occupation are found at Rhodes. This was the natural basis

[1] Meyer, *Alterthum*, I. 230.
[2] A number of Phoenician remains which were discovered in a grave at
Ialysos are preserved in the British Museum.

for their commercial operations in the Aegean; and though they traded to the coasts, they seem on the whole to have preferred to establish their settlements on the islands[1]; thus they occupied Cythera, Melos, Thera and Thasos, which gave them access to the Thracian coast, and furnished supplies of gold. At one or two points on the mainland they may have settled for a time, as at Corinth[2], at Thebes, and on the coast of Thrace ; while it is more than probable that they forced their way through the narrow channel of the Hellespont into the Black Sea[3]; the fisheries and wool-growing lands, as well as the iron mines, would tempt them thither, while they would also strike the line of the amber trade[4]. But they could not long preserve a monopoly in this quarter ; the Greeks soon learned to resist their depredations and to imitate their methods of seamanship and settlement. The decline of the supremacy of Sidon in Phoenicia seems to synchronise with the decline of Phoenician influence in the Aegean, as it gradually yielded to the aggressive enterprise of the Greeks.

But as the sphere of their operations was contracted on the north, the Phoenicians threw themselves with greater energy into their expeditions to the west. They had already made the long voyage from Crete to Sicily[5], and had found their way to

[1] Thucydides, VI. 2.

[2] Onka at Thebes is said by one Greek tradition to be a Phoenician goddess, and at Corinth the cults of Melicertes and Aphrodite have Phoenician characteristics. Meyer, *Gesch. des Alterthums*, vol. I. pp. 231, 234; Duncker, *Hist. of Ant.* II. p. 62.

[3] Meyer, *op. cit.*, I. 234.

[4] De Rougemont, *L'Age du Bronze*, p. 141. Amber was also brought across the Alps to the valley of the Po and the Adriatic.

[5] Kenrick, *op. cit.* 103. As a Phoenician centre Crete was only second, or perhaps equal, to Rhodes. There is no reason to suppose that they sailed deliberately into an unknown sea: not improbably their next step in advance was due to some accident, such as led in after ages to the discoveries of Wynland and of Brazil (*Growth of English Industry*, I. 90, 474). Such an occurrence is likely enough : but it was almost necessary to shape the course direct, as neither the African coast nor that of the

Sardinia and as far as Spain. Gades, which was a suitable port for fishing fleets and an excellent point for procuring the precious metals, was already settled before the time of Hiram ; it is the Tarshish to which Solomon was permitted to trade. But with the rise of Tyre, there was increasing activity shown in these westerly expeditions ; the Phoenicians are said to have passed beyond the Pillars of Heracles and established no fewer than "three hundred cities" on the African coast[1], while they occupied the southern coast of the Iberian peninsula at many points. It is not improbable, though it is not completely proven, that they actually sailed to Britain, and carried on mining in Cornwall.

The intermediate stretch of African coast at length began to attract them ; Utica and Hippo were established, and gave access to the caravan routes across the African desert. It was in this region that the greatest of the daughter-cities was established , Carthage, refounded perhaps in 814 B.C., was destined to eclipse the glories of Tyre[2].

26. Such was the area throughout which the Phoenicians established trading communications. The business they

Peloponnesus invited a coasting voyage. In the legend Daedalus is represented as flying from Crete to Sicily (Diodorus, IV. 77) ; Mount Eryx, on which the Phoenicians eventually retired when pressed by the Greeks, was one of the points which are associated with his name ; it has all the characteristic features of a Phoenician colony.

[1] Strabo regarded this report as incredible ; XVII. iii. 3.

[2] The legend of Carthage is briefly this. Pygmalion and Elissa were left to share the throne of Tyre, but the populace excluded the Princess, and she married Zicharbal, high-priest of Melcarth. Pygmalion became jealous and had Zicharbal assassinated ; Elissa headed a conspiracy of revenge, but found herself powerless in Tyre, and with her following sailed away ; from which circumstance she received the name of Dido, "the fugitive," according to the story. They settled at Cambe in North Africa, the site of an old Sidonian foundation, which had fallen into ruin by reason of its close proximity to the prosperous Utica ; the Tyrian foundation was known as Carthage "the new born." Lenormant and Chevallier, *Ancient History of the East*, vol. II. p. 186.

developed was to some extent a carrying trade between distant
countries, but they were also engaged actively in   Carrying and
importing materials and exporting manufactures   Active Trade.
for themselves.   The people of Israel catered for those who conducted traffic through their land, and dealt with them; but the
Phoenicians were men of enterprise who engaged in ventures
abroad.   At the same time it is clear that the Phoenicians
felt the full advantages of having a monopoly of trade, and took
active measures to prevent other merchants from having access
to the regions with which they carried on the most lucrative
business.   Their deliberate efforts to keep secret the sources
of their supplies of amber and of frankincense help to account
for the geographical ignorance displayed in earlier Greek literature.   The gruesome tales of the Laestrygones and Cyclopes,
and of the Symplegades—as well as those of Circe, Scylla and
Charybdis,—may not improbably have been largely invented
to deter the Greeks from sailing into the Black Sea, or to the
Western Mediterranean; the Greeks of later generations were
apt to stigmatise these fables as Phoenician lies [1].   The Carthaginians pursued a similar, exclusive policy in after ages, and
one of their ships unhesitatingly courted destruction rather
than guide the Romans to the Cassiterides with their mines of
tin.   This sort of jealousy was even felt within the circle
of Semitic communities, for in their most prosperous times the
Phoenicians refused to allow the Carthaginians to have access
to the mines of Tartessus.   By securing a monopoly, even of
articles which could be produced in any quantities, they would
be able to obtain a much higher price; this was the aim of the
Dutch in struggling for a monopoly of the East Indian spices.

There are other reasons which may render an exclusive
trade profitable, and these also may have weighed with the
Phoenicians in determining their policy.   So long as nearly
all navigation consisted of coasting voyages from port to port,

---

[1] Richter, *Handel und Verkehr*, p. 13.

there was an obvious advantage in maintaining the exclusive control of a route, and in thus being free from the danger of hostile attack. In later times the Mediterranean was divided into two areas, which were respectively the spheres of Greek and of Phoenician influence. We may see that it was in this way of paramount importance for Tyre to retain possession of harbours in Cyprus and Sicily; they gave her free access to the water-way. Much as she lost when she was driven from the Aegean, it must have been a more disastrous blow when the Greek conquest of Rhodes and of Crete closed important harbours to her, and severed the main arteries of her communications.

When examining the places with which they traded, and the objects of trade, we can see that the Phoenicians were definitely desirous, not only of finding a market for goods, but of supplementing the industrial resources of their own land. It has been pointed out that the facilities for commerce seem to have interfered with the development of native industries in Judaea—the people were content to purchase foreign manufactures; but the Phoenicians rendered trading facilities subservient to the development of industry. This has been already shown in indicating their relations with their neighbours in Syria, but it is equally clear in their maritime settlements. At some they were occupied in procuring pigments for dyeing, especially in fishing for additional supplies of the murex[1]. Iron and copper and tin were of use in the hardware trades; and it is not improbable that they obtained raw wool by sea as well as by land. The coasts of the Black Sea would afford ample supplies of this commodity[2], and the river valleys of the western side of Asia Minor were celebrated as grazing grounds from very early times. Varro records the legend that

[1] This was found off the coast of Boeotia, and near Cythera.

[2] On this and the other wool-growing regions of classical times compare Yates, *Textrinum Antiquorum*, 26.

sheep and goats were originally introduced into Greece by
Heracles, i.e. probably the Phoenicians[1]; when they were so
keen in obtaining dyes[2], they must have been anxious to
obtain a sufficient supply of materials for weaving[3].

It is sufficiently obvious too that much of their energy was
devoted to the importation of slaves. The opening chapter
of Herodotus gives a vivid picture of the manner in which
peaceful commerce might be suddenly changed into slave

---

[1] Varro, *De re rustica*, II. i. 6. It is not possible, however, always to
take Heracles as Phoenician. It may be better to interpret Heracles in
this case as a Pelasgian hero (Ridgeway, *Journal of Hellenic Studies*, XVI.
100), and to regard him as introducing sheep and goats into Arcadia in pre-
Achaean times. The early cult of Pan and Hermes (Yates, *Textrinum
Antiquorum*, 43) in this region would thus at least suggest that wool-growing and wool-trading were an important feature in the civilization of the
country in that primitive age. The diffusion of the worship of Pan from this
centre is not improbably associated with the diffusion of pasture-farming
as a trade, as e.g. at Tarentum in Italy. Grothe, *Wolle und Wollen-
manufaktur* in *Deutsche Vierteljahrsschrift* (Stuttgardt, 1866), IV. 290.
Myth and legend seem to show that there was a great development of
sheep-farming on the eastern coast of the Aegean. Mount Ida was the
place where Adonis and where Paris were occupied as shepherds; Marsyas
was a shepherd of Phrygia, and Arachne the inventress of spinning had
her home in Lydia (Grothe, *op. cit.* 279, 282).

[2] Richter, *Handel und Verkehr* 6. The purple dye was chiefly used
for woollen fabrics. One of the legends regarding the murex attributes the
discovery to a shepherd. H. Grothe, *op. cit.* 271.

[3] There is evidence to show that sheep-farming was carried on, on a
large scale, by the Greeks (*Od.* XIV. 100) and that they traded in wool
with the Phoenicians. The wool of Miletus is mentioned as an import into
Tyre in Ezekiel xxvii. 18 (*Sept.*). The Phoenician traders came with their
finished products and took in exchange from the islands and mainland of
Greece such commodities as hides, wool and slaves (Richter, *Sklaverei*,
p. 14: Beer, *Geschichte des Welthandels*, pt. I. p. 66). Coins struck by
Phoenicians at Salamis in Cyprus and elsewhere are found bearing a
sheep's head: the sheep was a sub-multiple of the ox, as silver of gold,
and the existence of a sheep-currency indicates the permanence and importance of this western wool-trade (cf. Ridgeway, *Origin of Currency*,
p. 272).

C. W. C.   5

raiding. He tells us how the Phoenicians "exporting Egyptian and Assyrian merchandise touched at various places ; when they arrived at Argos they spread forth their cargo, and on the fifth or sixth day from their coming several women came down to the sea-side....While these women were standing near the stern of the vessel and chaffering such wares as took most their fancy, the Phoenicians, shouting to one another, made a sally on them : the consequence was, that though most of the women made their escape, the sailors seized Io, together with a few others, threw them on board the vessel, and set sail for Egypt." Such conduct must have interrupted trading relations for the time, but where the Phoenicians had settlements, they were enabled to use them as depots for an organised commerce in slaves[1]. They were thus able to add steadily to the industrial population at Tyre[2]. The lot of these purchased slaves, imported from a distance, was doubtless harder than that of the servile population descended from the original inhabitants of Phoenicia, and it appears that they rose more than once in

[1] Rhodes, as the meeting-point of the routes from the Aegean and Crete, specially served this purpose. Meyer, *Alterthum*, I. 230.

[2] In pre-Homeric and Homeric times slaves could be acquired direct by war or piracy, or purchased from pirates and warriors. Spasmodic raids and surreptitious kidnapping gradually gave way to a more regular trade, in which Phoenicians, Cretans, Taphians, Lemnians, and Sicilians actively engaged (Richter, *Sklaverei*, pp. 13, 15), and incurred a certain amount of obloquy among Greeks on this account. Of this trade Rhodes, Crete, Chios, and Delos became centres. Slaves are recognised as staple commodities in Homer: e.g. in *Iliad* VII. 475 the Achaeans buy wine from Lemnians with captives among other things, and in *Odyssey* I. 430, XV. 482 Laertes is spoken of as acquiring a household slave for a certain price. In Herodotus II. 54 a woman from the temple at Thebes in Egypt was kidnapped by Phoenicians, and sold to the Greeks: and the inevitable consequence of defeat and capture by an enemy is slavery, with him or with a customer of his. It is easy to see that slaves trained in the arts and crafts of Phoenicia were worth much to the primitive and pastoral Greeks, and on the other hand to understand that Greek women and boys came to be reckoned of high value among "barbarians." Beer, *Geschichte des Welthandels*, I. p. 40.

successful insurrections[1]. Tyre made her commerce the means
of supporting manufactures, not merely by buying materials—
as many communities have done—but by purchasing and importing labour as well.

The character of Phoenician trade sufficiently indicates the
character of the Phoenician settlements; when we read of
three hundred cities on the African coast[2] we must think rather
of fortified factories than of regular colonies. Many of their
settlements seem to have been mere depots; though they had
some large colonies which served both as centres for trade
and as ports for the victualling and refitting of ships. Their
settlements in Rhodes, Cyprus, Sicily, Spain and Africa
were well provided in these respects; the inhabitants were
skilled in agriculture and devoted themselves to rural pursuits,
so that the colonies should not only be self-sufficing but well
furnished with stores. Along the line of Phoenician settlement, as it seems, the cultivation of the vine and of the olive
was introduced into European countries. But the inhabitants
of the trading factories would have no strong attachment to the
country where they lived; the readiness of the Phoenicians to
migrate is shown not only in the foundations of new colonies,
but also in their withdrawal before the Greeks.

27.   The prosperity of Tyre and its apparent security are
described in glowing language by the prophet   The Effects
Ezekiel[3]; he announced a sudden ruin, and we   of Commerce.
who look back can see that the foundations of its material
greatness were not firmly laid. Its power of resisting attack
depended on its wealth, for this gave the means of hiring
mercenaries; and its wealth was largely derived from its

---

[1] It has been suggested by Movers (*Phönizier*, II. i. 520) that such insurrections gave point to the remarks in Proverbs xix. 10, xxx. 22, and
Eccles. iv. 14, and x. 7.
[2] The trade at some of these points doubtless resembled that described
below. See p. 143, n. 4.
[3] Ezekiel xxvii., xxviii.

5—2

industry and skill in manufactures. But these had developed
to a pitch at which they could not easily be maintained; their
own ores and the nearest fisheries were partly worked out,
and the Phoenicians became dependent on foreign countries
for necessary materials, as well as for a supply of labour; a
temporary interruption of commerce meant the cessation of
many departments of manufacture. There were serious elements of instability inherent in such a community. Its splendid
situation enabled it to retrieve its prosperity once and again
after serious blows; but its story is none the less a significant
warning as to the concealed weakness of any great civilization
which is built "on the fluctuating basis of trade[1]."

It is to be noticed too that the great development of manufacturing at Tyre was incompatible with the planting and
growth of industries in the countries with which she traded.
Some of them, such as Judaea, might have little industrial
ambition, and might be satisfied with the rôle of an agricultural
community. But any people who cherished political ambitions,
or wished to attain to material prosperity by utilising the resources of their country themselves, would hardly care for intercourse with the Phoenicians. They were ready to work out
the minerals and to drain the population of other lands, so as
to accumulate still greater wealth in Tyre; the effect of such
commerce was to exhaust rather than to develop the resources
of the less civilised lands with which they traded.

We are inclined to assume in modern times that free commercial intercourse is sure to be beneficial to all parties who
engage in it, and that the distinction which was formerly drawn
between "gaining" and "losing" trades[2] is quite illusory.
But the story of the Phoenicians should at least give us pause;
we may come to see that it is important to consider the matter,
not only in regard to the actual exchanges made at a given
moment, but with reference to the ulterior and lasting effects
on the development of a country. It is true to say that there

---

[1] Cunningham, *Growth of English Industry*, II. 389.   [2] *Ib.* II. 127.

was an abnormal development of Phoenician industry at the
expense of other lands. Their factories conferred but little
lasting benefit; as miners, they worked at and worked out the
richer veins, leaving the district denuded of mineral wealth; as
fishermen, they seem to have exhausted the beds of the murex
they prized so much; as traders, they drained other lands of
a numerous and able-bodied population. The beautiful fabrics
and articles of luxury which they brought in exchange were
but a poor substitute for that which they carried away. They
enriched themselves; but their commerce tended to deprive
each of the other countries of the opportunity for self-development on all the various sides of life for which it was physically
adapted[1]. A sinister interpretation may be put on their readiness to retire before the Greeks; the Phoenician might not be
unwilling to withdraw from a land he had already despoiled of
its best.

There is another ground on which a still severer condem-
nation may be passed on the Phoenicians, despite their material
prosperity. They had great wealth, but they had no worthy
notion of using it. They seem to have had no political ambitions—such as the great monarchs of the East cherished; they
had low personal ideals and did not aim at giving scope for
the development of human life. Their imitations of Greek art
serve to show how incapable they were of appreciating it
aright[2]. To the wise man, wealth is but a means for the attain-
ment of nobler ends; they are but gross and vulgar barbarians
who treat it as an end in itself.

The strength and the misery of Phoenician civilization are
reflected in various aspects of the deity whom they recognised
as presiding over their destinies. Melkarth is the Heracles
of the Greeks, engaged in stupendous labours for the good of

---

[1] This principle has been worked out for modern times in the *National
Economy* of F. List. It underlies many of the current objections to the
principles of Free Trade.

[2] Renan, *Mission de Phénicie*, 827.

man ; overcoming countless obstacles and clearing the path of progress. But there is another side to the picture : Melkarth is but another name for Moloch[1],—a brute force demanding inhuman sacrifices in its triumph.

But with all their defects we yet owe a deep debt to the Phoenicians. Egypt had developed industry of nearly every sort[2]; in some few arts the Phoenicians made substantial progress, but their great claim to remembrance lies in the fact that they were the pioneers of maritime enterprise and colonisation in the Mediterranean lands; they gave an example for better men to copy. Nor should we be ungrateful for the warning which we may find in their fall : we may more readily note the inherent weaknesses and defects of a great industrial civilization which depends for its maintenance on the products of distant lands.

[1] Movers, *Phönizier*, I. 385.
[2] See above, § 8, p. 14.

BOOK II.

CHAPTER I.

GREECE AS CONNECTED WITH PHOENICIA
AND EGYPT.

28. WE look back to Greece as a land which has given us a heritage of Philosophy, Literature and Art; and so much stress is sometimes laid on these contributions to Western Civilization that some modern writers are liable to forget, or to under- rate, the debt we owe her in regard to our social and industrial life. There is an additional danger that we may err in this fashion after examining the story of her predecessors; the Egyptians and Phoenicians had done so much, that there seemed to be little scope for further advance; the elements of knowledge of all sorts—of agriculture and of textile arts, of metallurgy, and of ship-building—were consciously derived by the Greeks from the Phoenicians. We are apt to suppose that the industrial and commercial arts had reached, before the time of the Greeks, the level on which they stayed, till the ages of discovery in the fifteenth and of invention in the eighteenth and nineteenth centuries. This is to some extent true; but still the fact remains that the Greeks have left an indelible impress, not only on our intellectual and artistic, but on our industrial and commercial life. For though all the elements of material

The Greek Influence on Economic Life.

prosperity were developed before their time, the Greeks gave them a new character; they took a step towards solving the problem of reconciling the drudgery of labour with the liberty of the labourer. They realised that man's life does not consist in the abundance of the things he possesses; eager as they were in the development of commerce and the race for wealth, they treated material prosperity as a means to an end—an opportunity for the maintenance of political and intellectual life.

That the Greeks were quick-witted enough to improve on their masters in industrial arts and commercial enterprise is true; as sailors and ship-builders they gradually drove the Phoenicians from the seas in which they had been supreme: but their chief service lay in the fact that they introduced a new ideal of life, and pursued their commerce for more worthy ends. It has been pointed out above in regard to Egyptian history that the political and the economic sides of life can hardly be distinguished; the two sides, which we can study apart in modern life, were so intimately interwoven with one another. But the Greeks did learn to separate them; both in public and private life they distinguished between mere material prosperity and the personal self-development or political greatness, for which wealth provides the means.

It is in the clear consciousness of this distinction to which the Athenians of the age of Pericles had attained, that we see the inner reason of the superiority of Greek to Phoenician civilization; the distinction can be traced in earlier times, as for example in the contrast which may be drawn between Greek colonies and Phoenician factories. The cities which were founded on the east coast of Asia Minor, and the Greek colonies which were sent forth to more distant lands, were not mere trading stations that served to exploit and exhaust the products of the surrounding countries; they were new centres of civilising influence, and were from the first destined to be the homes of a free people. It was through the consciousness

of her mission to maintain and diffuse a higher conception of
the life of a free citizen, that Athens attained her glory as the
first home of a worthy civilization. At the period of her
greatest wealth, which was marked by the erection of the
magnificent public works on the Acropolis, she attained a
unique position in the cultivation of philosophy and art, and
all that makes life worth living.

It was possible for the Athenians to cherish these high
ideals, because they had taken a very important step in
economic progress and had become habituated to the regular
use of money. "Natural Economy,"—where men are bound to
one another by customary ties and discharge their mutual
obligations in service or in kind,—is quite compatible with a
stable and a prosperous life, but it offers serious obstacles to
social progress. The general introduction of money, and of
the opportunities for economic freedom which it brings with it,
is favourable to an advance in political thinking and in political freedom as well.

In a society where Natural Economy is dominant the
relations of persons and the exchange of things are so inter-
twined together that the picture we form of it is necessarily
blurred—we cannot apply familiar terms to describe it. But in
so far as the use of money permeates any community and is
taken for granted in its institutions, we are able to analyse the
true character of transactions clearly. It is not possible to say
of the serf, who renders service and enjoys a small holding of
land, whether he pays rent in service or receives wages in the
use of his arable plots. The two conceptions are blended ;
so too we cannot distinguish mutual gifts, or tribute, from commerce. The intervention of money renders the phenomena
more distinct ; in connection with modern public works, we
can distinguish between the pressure of taxation and oppression by government contractors ; where corvées are in vogue
the distinction can hardly be drawn. Where money enters in,
many transactions are set in clearer light ; they can be better

distinguished from one another and their mutual relations and importance can be perceived.

Money economy not only facilitates clear thinking, it also affords more opportunity for the individual to manage his own affairs in his own way. The main economic difference between the free man and the slave or serf, is that the free man works for the sake of reward, and the other under compulsion—the chief motive is different in the two cases. So soon as the reward is paid in money, the labourer is, to a greater extent, his own master; it becomes more a matter of choice whether he will work much for a larger reward, or whether he will be content with a smaller reward, and take it out in leisure. And economic freedom affords the conditions which render political freedom possible.

One fundamental characteristic of the free citizen is that he is a man with free time [1], which he can spare from manual tasks to devote to affairs, or to occupy with his own self-development in mind and body. In an age of payment by service or in kind, only the very wealthy [2] are possessed of free time; the more general introduction of pecuniary payments means that a larger proportion of the society are masters of their own time, and can, if they choose, enjoy some leisure for political life [3]. It was the fact that the use of money-bargaining

---

[1] Commutation of predial service for money payments in the fourteenth century did not give the mediaeval villeins the status of free men, but it made them masters of their own time.

[2] The grading of the duties of citizenship according to wealth has a good deal of justification in this conception.

[3] This, as Pericles boasted, was characteristic of Athenian citizens, Thucydides II. 40. The manner in which money economy gives the possibility for individual freedom is not sufficiently noted; when payment is made in rations and shelter the labourer's expenditure and place of habitation are determined for him; when he is paid in money he is free to spend it as he chooses. He need not necessarily be better off, but he is the master of his own earnings; the constant struggle against "truck" shows that the Englishman values this privilege. In exactly the same fashion it is true to say that the wage-earner may feel the pressure of

had permeated so many relations of life in Greece, that rendered the severance of political and economic affairs possible, and gave the opportunity for appreciating the relative importance of each.

29. The physical features of Greece gave her facilities for commercial industry; but they also afforded her   Physical an admirable opportunity for the development   Features. of free political institutions. Greece with its northern neighbours forms a remarkable series of peninsulas[1], and is well protected from an attack by land; she had far less to fear than the Phoenicians from the great monarchies of the East, and succeeded in repelling the invasions that were actually attempted. The barriers which separated one plain from another were in a sense a source of weakness: they rendered the fusion of the various states an impossibility, and interfered with the realisation of Greek unity: no Greek was ever at home in another Greek city than his own; he was even liable to be sold as a slave in a city in which he had no rights and no status[2]. Yet the very severance of the Greek states, and the smallness of the area of each, though in some senses a weakness, gave opportunities for their natural development. The cities in Greece proper had not been planted, they grew; and the conditions of limited area and easy communication were favourable to their self-development and independent growth. There was no one king of a united Greece, who could control the various civic communities, and interfere with them in working out their destinies.

At the same time, there was an underlying unity of race, and of something more than race. The various states lay so

poverty, but he is master of his own time and he has the opportunity of migrating to better himself, which the slave and the serf have not.

[1] Strabo VIII. i. 3.

[2] The story (Diog. Laer. III. 19, 20) of the sale of Plato as a slave, and his redemption, is at least an illustration of the personal insecurity of a Greek in any other city than his own.

close together that there was the possibility of frequent intercourse; and the shrine at Delphi was at least a centre from
which there issued occasional guidance. It served on more
than one occasion to strengthen the hands of a brave man in
entering on a bold course against the barbarians, and it helped
to determine the direction of colonial expansion.

There were definite material conditions, which had much
influence as well. "Greece looks towards the East." The
inhospitable shores of the western coast of Greece rendered it
impossible for the inhabitants on that side to take to a sea-
faring life; but on the east it was different. Harbours abounded, from which fishing fleets went out; and great colonising
expeditions started from them. The emigrants sailed forth to
the lands on the eastern side of the Aegean and founded the
Greek cities of Asia. From these in turn a series of colonies
emanated; looking towards the west the colonists sailed beyond their mother-country to western lands, and settled in
Italy and Sicily, and at Marseilles. With few exceptions the
stream of Greek colonisation followed this course; Corinth
almost alone was able to utilise her double-faced situation and
to feel her way to Corcyra and Illyria and the Adriatic direct.

It is important to call attention thus to the conditions
which were favourable for colonisation; for the greatness of
Athens was due to the fact that she was the leader in a confederation of maritime cities; it was as mistress of the Greek
seas that she attained her pre-eminence. But it must also be
remembered that her mineral resources played an important
part in enabling her to assume a supremacy in organising and
directing the energy of other states. Under her leadership a
combined front was maintained for a time; so that the Persians
failed to isolate the cities of Greece and attack them successfully in turn, as they had done in Phoenicia and Asia Minor.

Apart from these considerations of direct political importance, we may notice that the climate and soil of Greece
enabled the inhabitants to naturalise the rural arts which the

Phoenicians brought to their doors. The vine and the olive were cultivated with success; and the materials available for practising the mechanical arts were such that the pupils soon excelled their instructors. The Phoenicians had been great ship-builders, but the Greeks turned the woods of Thessaly to still better account, and as early as 700 B.C. built ships with three banks of oars. The Phoenicians had excelled as masons, but the quarries of Pentelicus furnished a marble in which the noblest architectural conceptions might be worthily embodied. There was no side of industrial development from which the Greeks were precluded by a lack of the material means for carrying it on.

For commerce also they were admirably situated. The Phoenicians had access to the southern caravan-roads to the East, and their cities formed depots for the trade with the West. The Greeks had trading connections with another caravan-route: the northern stream of commerce, from Persia and the Caspian, runs to Colchis and other points on the shores of the Black Sea; besides this, the amber and furs of the north found their way by the river-routes, and formed profitable articles of trade, from which the Phoenicians had been almost entirely cut off when they were driven from the Aegean. The Greeks had trading connections, not only with the north and east, but also with the south; for their factories in Egypt, and the planting of cities there [1], enabled them to open up a carrying trade which cut right across the line of Phoenician communications. That had run along the Mediterranean from east to west; but this led north and south from the Aegean by way of Crete to Egypt, and the wealthy lands which could be approached by the Red Sea.

30. Though there can be little doubt that the Greeks borrowed many of the arts of life from the Phoenicians, or from Egypt, we have but little direct evidence as to the precise channels of communication, **Links of Connection.**

[1] See above, § 14, p. 35.

or the extent of the debt. It is more than probable that the people of Cilicia[1], and their offshoots, took an important part as intermediaries between the cities of the Delta and the Greek peninsulas. For our present purpose, however, it is unnecessary to attempt to unravel the tangled web of conflicting evidence; it may be enough to point out that the fact of intercourse is abundantly established, though the precise nature of that intercourse at any time, or its duration at any place, can hardly be satisfactorily determined, as the information which has survived is so very fragmentary and slight.

From Phoenicia itself there is no direct evidence of any influence exercised on Greece in early times; though the existence of intercourse between the two antagonistic peoples is shown by the character of the later remains at Tyre, where there are abundant signs that the Phoenicians had become acquainted with Greek models and were trying to imitate them[2]. On the other hand, the Greek evidence is not easy to interpret; the earliest literature—the poems of Homer and Hesiod—gives a picture of Greek civilization at the time of the Trojan war, which cannot be easily reconciled with the remains recently disinterred at Mycenae, though these have been commonly regarded as the palace of Agamemnon. For one thing, the heroes of the *Iliad* were familiar with the use of iron; the people whose tombs have been recently examined were content to arm themselves with weapons of bronze. It is clear that either the literature has been edited, to accommodate it to the habits of a later age, or that the remains at Mycenae belong to a civilization of still earlier date than that of the Greeks who waged war against Priam[3]. We cannot assume that the literature and the remains refer to the same civilization alike; and archaeological remains, when entirely

---

[1] W. Max Müller, *Asien und Europa*, 346, 355.
[2] Renan, *Mission de Phénicie*, 827.
[3] Ridgeway, *Journal of Hellenic Studies*, XVI. 87.

divorced from literature and inscriptions, do not tell their own story with much precision. They are rarely self-interpreting.

Archaeological evidence does tell us something, however, as to the trading intercourse of different peoples in the ancient world; but the more it is examined the less does it afford the expected proof of Phoenician influence on the coasts of the Aegean. When we find a series of remains which show no vestiges of metals or commodities that were well known to other contemporary peoples, we may be confident that there was no regular and habitual trade between the two. It is quite unlikely that the inhabitants of the Troad, whose cities have been explored, had any regular dealings with the Phoenicians; the style of workmanship is so distinct that it is probable the two civilizations were not in regular communication. The gold ornaments found at Mycenae are also of a different character from the white gold which was most commonly available for the Phoenicians. This white gold or electron contained silver, which the metallurgists of early times were unable to separate out; but the gold of Mycenae is free from silver and is pure or red gold. It probably came from Thasos, Thrace and the Troad; on the whole, the remains suggest intercourse between the peoples of Mycenae and Hissarlik, but seem to show that neither of these cities procured gold from the Phoenicians, if they traded with them at all. The materials and the style of workmanship are alike against it.

On the other hand there is evidence, drawn from names and traditions, of the presence of Phoenicians in the Archipelago, especially in Thasos as well as in Boeotia and on the coast of Thrace. These were points within the pure-gold-producing area which the Phoenicians frequented, and where they established their cities[1]. Tradition also asserted that there had been a settlement of Phoenicians in Boeotia; and Herodotus ascribed to them the introduction of the alphabet,

[1] Herodotus II. 44.

as well as much other useful knowledge[1]. Even if he exaggerated
the precise extent of the debt in this particular case, the tradition of intercourse of this kind should not be lightly set aside.

It is confirmed moreover by the evidence of legend; the
legends of Heracles and Dionysus tell of the material benefits
conferred by intercourse with the Phoenicians, while that of
the Minotaur perpetuates the memory of their exactions. The
growth and popularity of the legends become intelligible when
we once recognise that they give us the poetic expression of
historical events. Because they are mythical they need not be
set aside as merely fabulous.

There is less difficulty in interpreting the evidence which is
furnished by numerous recorded incidents; even though we
are uncertain about the precise details of place, time and the
historic characters of the personages to whom they are attached, the narratives themselves may be taken as typical;
such is the story of a woman from Sidon[2] who had been
carried off by Taphian pirates, and in return stole her master's
son and escaped with Phoenicians, who had spent a whole year
in bartering at Syros.

There is frequent mention too of Phoenician wares, both
in the *Iliad* and *Odyssey*; they were evidently regarded as
superior to native manufactures. Sidon was famed for brass[3]
and for drinking cups in gold and silver[4], as well as for
"embroidered robes" which "shone like stars[5]." The Phoenicians may also have been intermediaries from whom the
Greeks of the day could have procured some Eastern or
African products such as ivory[6]. The incidental allusion in
the Homeric poems makes it sufficiently clear that the poets

[1] Herodotus v. 58.   [2] Homer, *Od.* xv. 415.
[3] *Od.* xv. 425.   [4] *Il.* xxiii. 741.
[5] *Il.* vi. 289, 295.
[6] *Od.* iv. 73; viii. 404; xix. 56. Phoenicia would be a possible but
not the only channel, and Caria and Lydia are specified in *Iliad* iv. 141 as
districts where working in ivory was carried on.

regarded intercourse with the Phoenicians, partly predatory and partly commercial, as a matter of course.

31. We have no literary evidence as to the life of the Greek peoples before they came under Phoe- nician influence, and hence have no means of gauging its precise effects; though some of the features set before us in early times could hardly be derived from Tyre. The picture which Hesiod gives us of a free cultivating peasantry has no parallel in what we can gather of the conditions in Phoenicia. The citizen farmer of Boeotia, in the seventh century before Christ, appears to have required one ox and one slave as the minimum stock on his land [1]; on better stocked farms [2] hired labour was employed, both male and female [3]. The descriptions of arable and pasture farming, as well as of the cultivation of the vine, in combination with occasional sea-faring, form a remarkable pic- ture; it seems to have been a hard life and one where constant diligence was required in order to get a living.

Primitive Conditions and Foreign Influ- ence. Coinage.

The Homeric poems are usually dated about a hundred years earlier, and they present us with a somewhat different picture; though the great households, which are there described, might well exist side by side with the smaller holdings of a free cultivating peasantry. These great lords had large house- holds and carried on pasture farming and arable farming and fruit farming simultaneously [4]; the work, both outdoor and indoor, was done by slave or servile labour; but the sons and daughters of the house were accustomed to share the duties. This fact shows that the number of slaves available was not very large after all, and that the position of the slave was not branded by any deep stigma of degradation; it was probably more comfortable than that of the poor freeman [5]. The

---

[1] *Opera et dies*, 405.   [2] *Ib.* 436.
[3] *Ib.* 602.   [4] *Il.* XIV. 122.
[5] Richter, *Sklaverei*, 20, 21.

household duties involved many kinds of work which have long since been undertaken as trades; the most arduous labour was that of the women grinding at the mill[1]; but a great deal of attention was also devoted to spinning and weaving[2], and this probably offered the best means of procuring by barter any necessary commodities which the estate did not afford. Such a household, with all its varied spheres of activity, was in the main self-sufficing, though some of the produce might be available for exchange.

A similar type of estate is found in many countries and in many lands, and there is no reason to believe that the establishments of the Homeric kings, as described to us, were anything but a native development. It is not improbable, however, that many of the arts of life as practised, at least latterly, in such establishments were of foreign introduction. The agriculture was not of a primitive type, as it was intensive in character, and the Homeric heroes were familiar with the manuring of land[3]. We have already noticed the existence of a tradition that sheep and goats were introduced from Africa, and this is probable enough; and the vine, on the culture of which Hesiod has much to say, was not indigenous. Within the households too, slaves, both male and female, would introduce unfamiliar arts. A great deal of knowledge has been communicated in this fashion at different times. The slaves of the Homeric period do not seem to have been very numerous, but they consisted of captives taken in war[4], or in piracy, and they would have every inducement to introduce

---

[1] Homer, *Od.* XX. 105.

[2] Richter, *Sklaverei*, p. 18. Grothe, *op. cit.*, 288. Compare also the woman in Proverbs xxxi. "She seeketh wool and flax, and worketh willingly with her hands (*v.* 13)....She maketh fine linen, and selleth it; and delivereth girdles unto the merchant" (*v.* 24).

[3] *Od.* XVII. 298.

[4] *Od.* I. 397. "But as for me, I will be lord of our own house and thralls, that goodly Odysseus gat me with his spear": in VIII. 523 a woman

better methods of carrying on industrial or domestic work, if it were only to lighten their own tasks and improve their status in the household.

In the other field of economic activity which Hesiod describes, the Greeks were undoubtedly debtors to the Phoenicians. The poet had less personal interest in sea-faring than in pasture farming[1], but he recognised its importance; he discusses the best seasons for sailing ventures, the size of the craft, and the necessity of laying up the ships during the winter with a view to preserving them from rotting. It is all the more a matter of regret that he tells us so little of the matter, as the analogy of later times would lead us to suspect that successful sea-faring was one of the arts by which men increased in wealth and status; and that the rise of the new nobility[2], and the knights, may be connected with mercantile success[3].

The Homeric poems give us more information as to the object and places of trade; whatever may be their value as historical evidence in regard to the events they describe, they certainly supply interesting illustrations of the habits of life at the time they were cast into final shape, or earlier. Iron was an imported commodity which the husbandman had to procure by purchase at a market[4], and articles of luxury of all sorts were obtained by maritime trade. In the Homeric poems, however, it would seem that the trade was merely "passive" so

is driven into captivity by her husband's slaughterers. In *Il.* XXIV. 734, Andromache foretells that her son will serve a ruthless master now that his father is dead: VI. 455, Hector foretells that his wife will be sent into slavery: "So shalt thou abide in Argos and ply the loom at another woman's bidding, and bear water from fount Messeis or Hypereia." Cf. Richter, *Sklaverei*, p. 13.

[1] *Opera et dies*, 650.

[2] Meyer, *Wirthschaftliche Entwickelung*, 25, 29.

[3] The law in Danish England that the merchant who fared three times over the sea should be of Thane-right worthy, is a case in point.

[4] *Iliad* XXIII. 834.

far as the Greeks were concerned, and that the merchants were
all Taphians, Phaeacians, Cretans or Phoenicians[1]. The Greek
adventurer by sea confined himself to piracy and plundering so
far as we can judge[2]. In this aspect there seems to have been
a distinct change of habit during the century which separates
the Homeric poems from those of Hesiod.

There is, however, evidence of an entirely different character, which throws light on the staple objects of trade at
different points in the Aegean; the Phoenician gave way
before the Greek, but the chief products of each area would
continue to be the staple of articles of trade, when it passed
into new hands. The characteristic features of classical Greek
civilization have been connected above with the recognition
of money economy as permeating all social relations, and it
is of special interest to note the first introduction of coined
money; it is also noticeable that when the types which are
found on the coins of various towns have a special character[3],
they give incidental evidence as to the principal objects of
trade.

We are so accustomed to the use of the precious metals as
a medium of exchange that it is not easy for us to recognise
that a trade in commodities might go on for centuries without
the intervention of money; there may be regular and organised
barter where some commodity that is commonly desired is
used as a unit, in terms of which the exchange value of other
goods is measured. In comparatively modern times fur skins
were used as units of value in America, and stock-fish[4] in
Iceland, and there is a high probability in the theory which

---

[1] Büchsenschütz, *Besitz und Erwerb*, 359.

[2] *Od.* IX. 40; XI. 401; XIV. 85, 262.

[3] The ox was so generally recognised as a unit of value among
commercial peoples (Ridgeway, *Origin*, 124), that we cannot infer the
existence of cattle farming from the use of this symbol on the coins of any
particular town.

[4] Ridgeway, *Origin*, p. 18.

derives the units of coined money from commodity-units that
were previously in vogue[1]. The slave-unit and the ox-unit
have on the whole superseded others that were merely local;
from them our English pound and shilling appear to be ultimately derived; but the natural products of each district seem
to have been used as the units in which bargains were struck
for the wares that traders from a distance brought with them.
Thus we have the tunny fish of Cyzicus[2], the silphium plant of
Cyrene[3], indicating staple products, while the double axe of
Tenedos[4], and the kettle of Crete[5] may not improbably be
derived from manufactured articles for which the locality was
highly celebrated. The coins came to be the representative
of the article which had at one time served as 'commodity-
money' in that place.

Such commodity-money, though possible, is not convenient.
The difficulty which is sometimes said to arise from the want
of "coincidence" in barter—each party having a thing to get
rid of, but neither being able to provide that which the
other wants—may not have been felt when maritime traders
with a varied selection of goods visited a coast in search of a
known product. But there might be a difficulty in defining
the quantity, and still more in describing the quality which
should be reckoned as a unit of value; no one slave is exactly
the same as another; they are not "homogeneous." The
superior convenience of metallic money, whether coined or no,
inevitably asserts itself sooner or later; and, according to their
own tradition, this was one part of the knowledge for which
the Greeks were indebted to the Lydians[6]. The earliest Greek

---

[1] Ridgeway, *Origin of Currency*, p. 49.
[2] *Ib.* 315.   [3] *Ib.* 313.
[4] *Ib.* 318.   [5] *Ib.* 314.
[6] Herodotus, I. 94. See the discussion in Rawlinson's *Herodotus*, I.
684. There does not appear to have been any native coinage among the
Egyptians, and the Phoenicians do not appear to have anticipated the
peoples of the Aegean in this matter.

coins seem to have been struck at Aegina[1], and for purposes of foreign rather than internal trade : yet so many persons were interested in commerce, that coins, when once introduced (700 B.C.), soon found their way into the transactions of ordinary life, and a century later, in the time of Solon, a money economy had almost completely superseded the natural economy of Homeric Greece.

32. If, as seems probable, the Greeks were consciously influenced by the Phoenicians in taking to maritime employments, it follows still more certainly that they imitated them in founding trading cities. The factories and colonies, which were planted on the coasts and islands of the Aegean, and later on the coasts of the Black Sea and the Western Mediterranean, closely correspond in their economic and industrial character to the settlements of the Phoenicians. There were differences in the stronger attachment to the mother city which the Greeks appear to have cherished, and in the antagonism to the barbarians which they shared, even when they had little else in common ; but the sources of their material prosperity were precisely similar to those on which the wealth of the Phoenician colonies was based. They were attracted by similar natural advantages in fixing on points for settlement, and the economic policy they pursued was not dissimilar.

Colonisation.

For our purpose it is unnecessary to consider the precise tribal affinities of different colonies—Ionic, Doric and Aeolic ; it will suffice to indicate very briefly their geographical distribution in the eighth century B.C. By this time the foundation of Greek cities on the coasts and islands had gone so far that the Aegean might be regarded as a Greek sea, and a stream of emigration was directed into the lands beyond. In these expeditions Miletus took the lead ; its ample supply of wool[2] enabled it to rival Tyre in the manufacture for which it was

---

[1] Ridgeway, *Origin,* 216.
[2] Curtius, I. 410; Grothe, *op. cit.,* p. 280.

famous, and the merchants of Miletus were eagerly engaged in procuring additional supplies of products, which might subserve the further development of industry. At first, temporary fairs on the coast were held; the places on the shore were pur- chased by treaty from the inhabitants; fixed market places with storehouses were erected, and agents of the mercantile houses established in them; they superintended the landing and sale of the goods, and remained abroad even during the suspension of navigation in winter. Some of these stations were subsequently relinquished. Others, the situation of which proved favourable on account of mercantile advantages, or the excel- lence of climate and water, were kept up and enlarged; finally, a depôt of wares grew into an independent trading place, a Hellenic community and an autotype of the mother city. It was in this way that the men of Miletus founded new cities at Abydus and Cyzicus, so as to command the Dardanelles and to have an excellent depôt on the Sea of Marmora. Their next step was still more important, for the city of Sinope, founded in 785 B.C., gave them access to most valuable pro- ducts; not only to food supplies, of corn and the tunny fish, and excellent timber for shipbuilding, but to quantities of iron ore, as well as red lead, a rare and precious material in the ancient world; while they could also obtain large consignments of slaves. From this point there was a gradual movement eastward along the coast of the Black Sea; Trapezus gave access to gold fields, Phasis to trade with Armenia and the East, while Tanais and Olbia formed depôts for the products which came from northern lands down the great rivers.

Another group of colonies was established by Chalcis, a city which was specially devoted to hardware trades; the men of this town made settlements in the mining regions on the coast of Thrace, and were before long brought into hostile relations with the Milesian colonies on the Dardanelles. But they also turned their energies in a very different direction; they traded with the Peloponnesus and Crete, and thus pushed

their way up the Adriatic to Corcyra, a new centre from which
the cattle and other products of Illyria soon became the objects
of a busy trade; while the members of the same group of
colonies were also among the first to find their way to the
Italian mainland and to settle at Cumae[1]. Rhegium was built
as a harbour of refuge on the straits; and soon afterwards the
struggle between the Greeks and Phoenicians entered on a
new phase, when the cities of Naxos and Syracuse were
founded in Sicily. It is unnecessary to dwell on the number of
settlements which subsequently arose on the Gulf of Tarentum
and converted that fertile region into Magna Graecia, or to
enumerate the steps by which Greek influence extended more
and more in Sicily. It may suffice to call attention to the
farthest point of Greek colonisation, which was reached by the
Phocaeans when they settled at Marseilles in 600 B.C.

There is also much that is of interest in the new relations
with Egypt which were springing up at this time. The Phoenicians had never been able to plant a colony there, and the
Greeks were long confined to mere smuggling; though the
Milesians at length secured a factory at Canopus, to which
their operations were strictly confined; but during a revolution
in 630 B.C. they were able to establish themselves forcibly, and
subsequently to secure royal favour and protection at Naucratis.
It is at this point that we see most clearly the reaction of
Greek civilization on that of older lands; they forced Egypt to
become a centre for maritime trade, and to make the mouth of
the Nile the depôt for commerce between East and West.

The similarity between the commerce of the Greeks and
that of the Phoenicians is plain enough; but there were differences which are worth noting. The Greeks did, as a matter of
fact, bring with them their Hellenic civilization, and plant it in
the new lands. The cities of Sicily and Southern Italy were a
Greater Greece beyond the seas. The Greeks came, as the
Phoenicians had rarely done, not merely to exploit a country,

[1] Curtius, I. 438.

but to settle in it and develop its resources; while they were able to secure a permanent footing even in countries where they had no extent of territory, but merely a staple town for commerce, as was the case at Naucratis[1]. Nor did any antagonistic race arise for centuries to cause the withdrawal of the Greeks, as they themselves had ousted the Phoenicians; to whatever circumstances it may be due, the Greeks not only came to trade, but to stay. The permanence of this Greek influence was favoured by the effect of Alexander's conquests, and to some extent by the policy which was deliberately pursued from Rome; but there was an inner reason also. The bond of attachment to the mother city was a very real thing, which affected not only the religion and the politics, but the trading habits of the colonies. So to speak, particular grooves of navigation were formed in the sea, from one commercial place to another. It was as if one could start from no port besides Miletus in order to proceed to Sinope, and from Phocaea alone in order to reach Marseilles[2]. The tie of affiliation was strongly felt in the cities of the Middle Ages, and was of importance with regard to the definition of the privileges enjoyed, and the interpretation of local customs; among the Greek cities the tie was far deeper, and strengthened in a sense of being the emissaries of civilization against barbarism.

33. After all, the Greeks were united by something more important than a common antagonism to the barbarian; they were bound together by the ties of religion, which may serve sometimes as a bond between tribes that have little outward or political unity. One such instance is found in India to-day; whatever the government may be in any district, society is everywhere formed under Brahminical influence on the same model, and the economic structure is similar throughout. A similar state of things

The Oracle and Hellenism.

[1] Curtius, I. 426.
[2] *Ib.* I. 411.

existed formerly in Christendom; in the Middle Ages all the
rival towns and principalities of Western Europe formed part
of a religious whole, and were to some extent controlled by the
ecclesiastical potentate at Rome. In much the same fashion
the destinies of Hellenic influence were superintended and
guided by the priests at the Delphic temple; the oracle was
the mouth through which they gave authoritative, if uncertain,
guidance; and on more than one occasion oracular response
had a marked effect on the fortunes of Greece. The persistent
directions to begin and to develop a settlement at Cyrene[1]
and the utterance delivered before the battle of Salamis may
be quoted as cases in point[2].

The priests at Delphi, in frequent intercourse as they were
with Greeks from all parts of their world, were well informed
as to the course of events, and were in an admirable position
for forming a wise judgment on current affairs. They may in
this respect be compared to the Curia in Papal Rome. In
the period of Athenian greatness the priests at Delphi commanded another source of power, as the wealth laid up in their
treasury was so great that they were able to finance any project
in which they were keenly interested[3].

Amid much that is similar between the oracle and the
curia, both in their policy and the causes of their decline,
there was one marked difference in the aims and policies of
the two theocratic powers. Western Christendom formed a
continuous area of land in which naval intercourse played but
a little part; it was the work of the church to put down
private war and to establish the peace of God on land. The
conditions among the Greeks were very different, for their
cities were severed from one another, or we may say connected, by the sea; it was necessary to place such settlements in such a way that the sea-routes should be kept open

---

[1] Herodotus, IV. 150—159; Müller, *Doric Race*, I. 285 seq.
[2] Thirlwall, II. 326.
[3] Curtius, II. 41.

for coasting vessels, and also to give security to mariners. A glance at the map shows how successfully the former object was attained, and it is also true that sedulous efforts were made to expel the Phoenicians from the Aegean, and to destroy nests of pirates wherever they were found[1]. The established custom as to right between shipmen and traders may in some of its parts be older than the days of the Greeks, but the earliest form in which it can be traced is connected with the name of Rhodes. All subsequent arrangements for commercial security can be traced back to the time when the Greeks established their Aegean settlements and thus attained to a sovereignty at sea.

[1] The Athenians took a leading part in putting down piracy, though they were of course accustomed to organise privateering expeditions in time of war. Beauchet, *Droit privé de la République Athénienne*, IV. 365.

CHAPTER II.

CITY LIFE.

34. GREEK life, at the time when Athens had taken a lead in repelling the Persians and had attained the zenith of its prosperity as an influence in the world, was a city life; it was the period when the city-state was seen at its best. In the earlier history of the Greek peninsulas there had been the households of the Homeric kings, and the homes of a free yeomanry, such as Hesiod describes. But when the Phoenician influence had really been brought to bear, and after it had produced its full result, we see another type of social organisation in the same country. We find independent cities, like Athens, inhabited partly by resident aliens, but very largely by free citizens both rich and poor. Athens resembled Tyre in many ways, especially in its independence of political superiors; but it also differed fundamentally, since it afforded conditions and opportunities for the free political life of the individual citizens. This last feature has been already alluded to; but the point is of such importance that it is worth while to examine some of the characteristics of Greek city life in greater detail, and to indicate the economic conditions which they presupposed. It is only in this way that we can see the real nature of the Greek contribution to economic and social progress.

The City as an Economic Whole.

It has been pointed out above that the oppressive subjection of the Egyptian population to the Pharaohs is at least
partly accounted for by the control which the rulers had over
the means of irrigation and the consequent food supply. A
population that is economically dependent[1] for the means of
life can hardly expect to be politically free. This was obvious
in some of the palace-cities and military cities of antiquity;
if a mass of people has to be regularly maintained and fed
by provisions that are fetched from the surrounding country
or a distance, the necessary supplies may be obtained authori-
tatively and forcibly as a tribute. When an army establishes
itself in a fort and plunders the surrounding country, or when
a king builds a fortified palace and draws contributions from
his provinces, the city life may be maintained on the spot
so long as the army holds its own, or the royal power is
maintained. But such a city has no stable economic basis,
and has therefore no element of permanence as a community;
political changes may bring about the subversion of the ruler
on whose authority its very existence depends. A change of
dynasty may lead to the desertion of the old for a new palace
on an unoccupied site ; and the old city may become in a very
brief period a scene of desolation like the countless ruined
cities of Assyria and India.

The commercial or industrial city enjoys a very different
position ; it has, not its own food, but the means of procuring
a sufficient supply, within itself; it is safe against decay,
because it obtains the necessary sustenance for its inhabitants
indirectly from its own resources ; because its own activity
either as a commercial depôt or a manufacturing centre,
enables it to give as good as it gets. Hence the commercial
and industrial city is a type of social organisation which shows
a high degree of vitality. It may maintain itself for many

[1] When the food supply is procured from other countries in the course
of trade, the case is altered; there is a more or less stable basis of independence in the products or manufactures with which food is bought.

centuries as Cadiz and Marseilles have done; or it may rise
again on the same site after it appeared wholly dead, as seems
to have been the case with London and some of the other
cities of Roman Britain. The economic bases on which such
city life rests are not immutable, but they may be very firm,
and the economic institutions of city life persist in reappearing
from age to age. The city may be defined for economic
purposes[1] as an aggregate of households, which are united
by common ties and common interests, but each of which is
economically distinct from the others. Buying and selling
takes place between the households in a city, as it does
not between the members of a household or of a primitive
village. Hence in any city, where a large proportion of the
inhabitants are free citizens and money economy is in vogue,
there may not only be political independence for the city,
but political freedom within it. The citizens are not bound
by customary obligations discharged by customary contributions, but they are free to buy and sell and bargain with
one another, and are to a considerable extent independent
of each other.

The influence of the introduction of money in facilitating
personal independence[2] has often been overlooked, and it is
necessary to lay stress upon its importance as exhibited in
Greece. The substitution of money taxation for the personal
rendering of service to the state is one considerable step

[1] The terms *country* and *nation* have to be defined differently for economic and for political purposes in modern discussion (*Modern Civilization*,
p. 92), and we need to draw the same sort of distinction in the use of the
term *city*. In the following pages the term 'city' is used in its economic,
rather than its political or religious sense. Cf. Fustel de Coulanges, *Cité
Antique*, III. iv, v, vi.

[2] Modern Socialism exhibits a tendency to try and supply a substitute
for money transactions and thus to get rid of the evils of competition; but
it is to be noticed that this change would remove the conditions on which
all personal independence has rested in the past; it is difficult to see how
it could be safeguarded in the future.

in this direction; the man who is bound to render work of
any kind is necessarily astricted to some region where he may
be found and called on when required; the man who pays
taxes is free to move, so long as his property is within reach,
and can be claimed for public purposes. The accumulation
of hoards of wealth in the form of money and the introduction
of capital have a similar effect on industry. The labourer who
has no money must work at the thing he knows, and he can
most easily train his child to follow his own calling; under
a natural economy, change of employment is difficult if not
impossible. But the capitalist, who has a hoard of wealth
which he can realise in money, can embark in a fresh field
of enterprise that seems likely to be profitable, or can easily
vary the methods in which the business is carried on ; the introduction of capital—accumulated wealth which is realisable
in money—facilitates change of employment. The introduction of money has similar effects on the relations between
master and man. When payment is made in kind, in return
for service rendered, the labourer has little choice as to the
form in which he will take his earnings, and no choice as
to the time of labour; when he works for wages he is free
to choose his own way of spending his earnings, and free
to decide whether he will work on the terms offered and for
the time specified, or no. This is a step in advance because
it opens up possibilities of progress, and of rising in the
world, though the wage-earner does not necessarily enjoy
increased comfort. The slave may enjoy more food and
better clothing than the free man earns; but the one is incited to work by the fear of punishment and the other by hope
of reward. Hence the removal of disabilities gives no immunity from poverty and starvation, though it makes a man
master of himself. Freedom to migrate, freedom to change
employment, freedom to work or not and to spend what he
earns as he likes, are important elements in personal independence ; and these only become possible as the consequences

of the introduction of money taxation, the capital of moneyed men, and the payment of wages in money. In the Athens of the time of Pericles these conditions were so far introduced and a considerable number of the inhabitants had secured such economic independence, that they were able to enjoy a personal political freedom, such as was impossible in the ancient Egypt or in Phoenicia.

35. Some cities have been deliberately planted for military or administrative reasons; and so soon as commerce was developed, it became important to lay out cities which should be depots of trade; this motive has been at work in many ages; in the foundation of Tyre, of Phoenician and Greek colonies, of Alexander's cities, and the *bastides* of Edward I. Other towns appear to have sprung up, without definite design, as circumstances favoured them; and when we study them, we may detect the nature of the centre round which the dwellings were placed; it may have been a religious shrine, or a military fort, or merely a market-place. The ground-plan of a town that has grown,—so different from the rectangular lines of towns that were laid out,—may sometimes reveal the nature of the attraction which led men to frequent that particular site[1]. Athens may be classed as a town that grew up naturally[2]; and though we may not be able to discriminate its precise nucleus with any certainty, we can understand some of the causes which led to its being frequented by a large population which was economically free.

Athens as a typical indigenous Greek city.

---

[1] Compare the main streets of Norwich circling round the castle moat, and the older streets of Carlisle conforming themselves to the triangular market-place. Of course both conditions combine; the existence of a castle would bring trade to the market.

[2] Kuhn, *Entstehung der Städte der Alten*, 160. It is possible that the beginning of city life in Attica was due to a desire for mutual protection against the raids of pirates. The dread of invasion drove the citizens from the country to inhabit the city in 431 B.C. (Thuc. II. 14—16). Compare also the derivation of *oppidum* from *ob, pedum.*

It is evident from the political history of Athens that it contained a large number of poor citizens; many of these were doubtless men, or the descendants of men, who had found the hard life of a yeoman farmer unprofitable, and had been forced to leave the land and seek a living in the town. Others were men of alien extraction who were resident in Athens; they had no political power, and no personal political duties, though they were compelled to pay a tax. For all business purposes they were on an equality with the citizens; their numbers were greatly swelled, after the improvement of the harbour at Piraeus by Themistocles[1], when the commercial facilities and industrial development of the town made it attractive to men of enterprise, who in turn promoted its prosperity by their exertions. It appears that the greater part of the industrial work in Athens itself was carried on by wage-earners; there were some factories in which slave labour was employed[2], but on the whole it seems that slaves were chiefly engaged in rural occupations and in mining, and that the greater part of the Athenian artisans were economically free. This economic freedom of the townsmen, as compared with the more restricted conditions in rural districts, would in itself prove an attraction, and bring about a trend of the citizens towards the city.

After all, this was only the material condition of the social privileges which the Greeks prized. The strong attraction exercised by towns in the present day is a matter of frequent remark, for the town as a place of human intercourse offers advantages which the rural districts never afford. This distinction was more striking in bye-gone times; nowadays eyes trained in the artistic faculty, which the painting and sculpture of many ages have developed, come to appreciate the beauty of natural scenery, and the printing-press brings

[1] Grote, v. 337.
[2] Like that of Polemarchus and Lysias, who made shields and employed 120 slaves. Grote, VIII. 336.

learning and news within the reach of those engaged in rural occupations,—in fact, there has been a reaction of town culture upon the inhabitants of the country districts. But in ancient times it was not so; the town remained the centre of intellectual activity, where the peculiarly human pleasure of good talk could be enjoyed,—where learning of all sorts might be acquired, and graciousness and courtesy of character developed. Dr Johnson's complete appreciation of the delights of London life is an eighteenth century illustration of the grounds of the attachment of Greeks to their cities; more especially attractive was the glamour of life in Athens, where cultivated city habits attained their highest development[1].

This glorification of cultivated human intercourse as the ideal life, to which all else should be subservient, is the mark which distinguishes Greek from Phoenician culture and influence. In all the mechanical arts and the conduct of business the Egyptians and Phoenicians were first; they too had commercial cities; they had all the magnificence and all the luxury which were available for the Greeks. But they never attached such value to human life and personality as the Greeks did; their human sacrifices and the torture of their unsuccessful generals marked them out as barbarians. The best Greeks cherished an ideal of humanity, and material prosperity fell into its due place as a means to an end.

Doubtless the Greek ideal was limited in its scope; doubtless man has learned to frame wider conceptions of civilized life; he has made progress too in securing power over the means of realising them. But the struggle between the principles which the Greek and the Phoenician respectively represented, has never ceased. Whenever we find a pursuit of material wealth for its own sake, instead of as a means to an

---

[1] The depreciation of the countryman is clearly seen by the meaning attached to ἀστεῖος as opposed to ἀγροῖκος: the same opposition appears in Latin between *urbanus* and *agrestis, rusticus, vicanus*.

end[1], or the destruction and degradation of human life in the
march of material progress, we see what is alien to the Greek
spirit.   While we are grateful for all the heritage of ingenuity
and artifice which we have received from the Phoenician and
the Jew, we must strive to recognise continually that wealth
was made for man, not man for wealth, so that our ideals
of life may not fall below the standard that was set in Greece.

36.   An attempt has been made above to show that it is
essential for the political independence of a city,   The Food
that it should have the command of a sufficient   Supply.
food supply; in Athens, special pains were taken to provide that
the supply should be abundant, and that the inhabitants should
have the advantage of cheap food.   Solon was anxious to
develop industrial life at Athens and to attract immigrants who
should make it their permanent home[2]; it was therefore part
of his scheme of policy to prohibit the exportation of corn, so
that the Athenians might have exclusive rights to purchase
corn raised in Attica ; but even before his time it is probable
that a portion of the food supply was drawn from abroad.   At
all events the restrictions on export and the competition of
foreign grown wheat in the Athenian market must have told

---

[1] For a justification of the pursuit of riches compare Xen. *Oec.* XI.
Ischomachus had no small care to provide himself with riches in order to
be able to serve the gods, to serve his friends, and to help the city.   He
expressed contempt (c. XIV) for men who out of covetousness care not
what they do, nor what indiscreet means they take, so that they gather
riches together, but thought that those who increased their fortunes with
discretion and good judgment and became serviceable to the city, should
be esteemed wise and generous (c. XI).   The attitude taken by Cato—as
the ideal Roman of the good old times—is instructive from the contrast it
affords; he held "that the man truly wonderful and godlike, and fit to be
registered in the lists of glory was he, by whose accounts it should at last
appear that he had more than doubled what he had received from his
ancestors" Plutarch, 21 (Langhorne).   Cato lived up to his own creed,
both by his usurious transactions and by his success in training and dealing
in slaves.

[2] Plutarch, *Solon*, 22, 24.

severely against the agricultural interest; they would go far to neutralise the benefits which other parts of Solon's legislation were intended to confer on the cultivating peasantry.

The depressed condition of the yeoman farmers, at the time when Solon came into power, was not in all probability due to any special circumstances or laws; there was a sufficient reason for it in the fact that agriculture had come to be pursued as a trade with reference to a market, and was no longer chiefly directed to supplying the requirements of the cultivator's household; money economy had taken the place of natural economy. The farmer procured advances in money to enable him to carry on his business, and he took his produce to market to sell for a price; the peasant farmer has difficulty in adapting himself to such conditions, as he is forced to do, if he has to pay rent, or taxation, or interest, not in kind but in money. It would appear that in Solon's time rents in Athens were to some extent paid in kind[1], and there is no reason to suppose that a land-tax existed; but the wealthy men, on whom the poor peasant is often forced to rely for occasional help, made advances in silver, and on the security of the debtor's land[2]. This practice is in itself a serious thing for the poor cultivator; if advances are in the form of seed, on the security of the coming harvest, there is less danger of the debt being carried over from year to year, and accumulating to an amount which renders redemption hopeless[3], but this may easily occur when the debt is in silver and secured on the land.

Whenever a particular demand for money comes upon the poor cultivator,—from capitalists, landlords, or tax-gatherers,— it compels him to revolutionise his whole economic habits. He is bound to obtain money and thus he is compelled to

---

[1] This is a fair inference from the mention of the ἐκτημόριοι. Plut. *Solon*, 13. Compare also Boeckh, *P. E. A.* II. 12.

[2] Plut. *Solon*, 15.

[3] This change is said to have had a disastrous effect on the position of the ryots in British territory in India.

sell his produce for money. This may be a disadvantage in
many ways ; in good seasons, when the price is low, he cannot
afford to store a surplus and make provision for bad years ; he
must realise in money; in bad years, he will have nothing to
fall back upon, and if he has any crop to sell, it is quite likely
that foreign importation will render it impossible for him to
take full advantage of a famine price.

From the remedies applied by Solon, it is easy to see that
the cultivating peasantry of Athens had succumbed before the
difficulties of this economic revolution.   Even under the natural
economy, which may have existed in the time of Hesiod, the
farmer's lot was hard ; but the pressure of the demand of
moneyed men rendered it intolerable.

Solon's celebrated legislation was intended to relieve the
poor citizens, and it was directed against the money-lenders[1].
It cancelled existing debts, and may in all probability have
appealed to the common sense of justice.   If a large amount
had been paid as interest, there was no grave injustice in
striking off the principal,—the money-lenders may have already
received 100 per cent. on what they advanced,—while it was
now made impossible for them to lend on the security of the
citizen's person.

From the subsequent history it is clear enough that the
agricultural interest was not permanently relieved.   The cultivating peasantry must have been involved in difficulties as
great as ever, or even greater.   As they could only give inferior
security, they may have had to pay higher rates of interest
than before; the business of the farmer was not more profitable than it had been, and Solon's measure could not avert the
ruin of the cultivating citizens.   He prevented them from being
ousted by their creditors ; instead of lingering on hopelessly,
they would be forced to sell their land and to give up the
struggle before it had become desperate.   As we know, the
immediate effect of Solon's legislation was to give some moneyed

[1] Grote, III. 139.   Compare the Deccan Relief Bill of 1880.

men the opportunity of buying large estates[1]. It has been said
that Solon's legislation never had to be repeated[2], and this is
true ; but the commonly assigned reason is mistaken. He did
not succeed in saving the peasantry, for the class he tried
to protect were driven from their holdings, not as slaves, but
as bankrupt freemen. The ruined yeomen found employment
as stewards, or they went to swell the crowd of wage-earning
citizens at Athens ; while the lands they had relinquished were
worked as large farms by enterprising Athenians, who were
able to employ a troop of slaves.

We thus find that peasant farming in Attica gave place
gradually to those large estates of the management of which
Xenophon has given us an inimitable picture in his *Oeconomi-
cus*. Without assuming that there was any great superiority
in the methods or implements employed, as compared with
those that were available in the *petite culture*, we can see from
Xenophon's tract how the larger holder could work at a profit.
The whole of his internal management was based on natural
economy ; his slaves grew food for themselves, and for the
requirements of the master's household ; no money passed, and
the consideration of price did not directly enter. The pressure
on the agricultural interest may have resulted in making the
work of the slaves more arduous, and their rations smaller,
but there is no reason to suppose that their masters lost money.
On the other hand, they could devote their land to the production of the most profitable articles,—such as fruit and other
commodities for which there was little competition in the
Athenian market, as well as the olives which the farmer was

[1] Three friends of Solon are alleged to have availed themselves of the
economic disorder to borrow money and buy up lands under mortgage at a
cheap rate : by some Solon himself was implicated in the transaction, but
Aristotle has cleared him. Arist. *Ath. Pol.* 6 : Plutarch, *Praecepta geren-
dae Reipublicae*, 807.

[2] The allegation that he debased the currency in the interest of debtors
appears to be disposed of by the *Constitution of Athens*. See Ridgeway,
Origin of Currency, p. 305.

permitted to export. The tendency would be to discourage
the growth of corn, except in so far as it was needed for the
proprietor's household, including the slaves on his estate, and
to encourage other kinds of cultivation instead. Hence it would
seem that the Athenian market became more and more dependent on the supplies of corn which were imported from abroad.

We may now turn to consider the regulation of the food
supply, in so far as it was drawn from distant lands. The
Athenians were at considerable pains to protect the course of
the corn-ships; convoys were sent with the fleets, and Sunium
was fortified to protect the corn-ships sailing under the pro-
montory. Nor were these precautions unnecessary; the enemies
of Athens were well aware how easily she could be injured by
cutting off the supplies of corn. This was abundantly illustrated during the Peloponnesian war[1], and Philip of Macedon
tried to obtain possession of Byzantium[2], with the view of
interrupting the supplies from Pontus. Athens was not dependent on any one source of supply, however, as grain was
imported from Pontus, Thrace, Syria, Egypt, Libya and Sicily.
Still it was no easy thing to give adequate protection to vessels
which came from so many diverse quarters.

There was some difficulty in securing that the merchants
should ship corn to the Piraeus, and not to other ports. They
were inclined to enquire how prices ranged at the different
places where they might take their cargo, and to select the
market that seemed likely to offer the best sale[3]. One method
of guarding against this, and compelling the shippers to bring
the corn to the Piraeus, was exemplified in the law which provided that money should not be lent on bottomry upon any

---

[1] Athens was able to hold out even when she could no longer pretend
to resist Sparta by land, but the naval victory of Lysander at Aegospo-
tomi, left her a prey to famine and proved a crushing blow (Grote, VIII.
301). See also Xen. *Hell.* v. iv. 61 and Diod. Sic. xv. 34.

[2] Demosthenes, *De Corona*, 87. ?54.

[3] Xenophon, *Oec.* xx.

vessel which did not bring a return cargo to Athens[1]; this proviso seems to have had special reference to the corn-trade, and Athenians were prohibited from shipping corn elsewhere[2]. The ships which arrived were obliged to sell two-thirds of their corn in Athens; only one-third was available for re-exportation.

These expedients for obtaining a plentiful supply were frustrated, to some extent, by the action of wholesale dealers in Athens; they bought up the corn when it arrived, and retailed it afterwards at excessive prices. These middlemen made high profits, which would not have been grudged if they had gone to the importing merchants, but, as it was, seemed to be earned by mere extortion. Many measures were passed to limit their operations[3]; the amount which they might purchase was limited to fifty loads, and they were compelled by law to sell again at a price which only allowed a moderate return on the sum paid. In order to enforce this "assize of corn[4]" officials (*sitophylaces*) were appointed to keep an account of the imports of corn and the prices at which it was sold. There were also public granaries at Athens in which corn was stored. It is possible that they were of the nature of bonding warehouses, where merchants could stow their corn, so as not to be compelled to sell their cargo off at the rates which ruled when their ships arrived; there seems, however, to have been

[1] See Boeckh, I. pp. 77, 78.

[2] Dem. *Adv. Phorm.* p. 918; *Adv. Lacrit.* p. 941.

[3] "Engrossing" beyond the limits of the law was punished by death— the dealers, according to Lysias, would be insufferable without this menace. The magnitude of the penalty emphasizes the paramount importance which the Athenians attached to their corn supply, and at the same time reveals a somewhat brutal severity in the treatment of a class which consisted chiefly of resident aliens. Lysias, *Adversus Frumentarios*, p. 715 et seq.; Boeckh, I. p. 111 et seq.; Mahaffy, *Social Life in Greece* (3rd ed.), p. 403 et seq., where the attacks on corn-dealers in the Middle Ages in seasons of scarcity, and likewise in Italy in 1874, are compared.

[4] The settlement of the prices of bread or ale by public authority was known in medieval England as an assize.

a public stock of corn, to which contributions were occasionally made by wealthy citizens, and from which food was sold on easy terms, or even given, to the poorer citizens. The pauperising effect of such distributions of corn is commonly spoken of in the history of Rome, but it also had an important bearing on the fortunes of Athens.

It is extremely interesting to observe how the Athenian authorities dealt with the problem of securing a sufficient food-supply for an industrial and commercial city. The difficulties recurred in subsequent times, and it is to be noticed that the expedients they tried, for checking the operations of middlemen and for forming public granaries, were afterwards adopted in English towns[1]. There is every likelihood that they were freshly devised to meet the old difficulties, when these arose in a new land; but Athens gives a type of city organisation which never became extinct in Europe, during all the changes of Roman conquest and barbarian invasion.

37. Such were the economic conditions which rendered the political independence of Athens possible; we must now turn to consider the internal condition of the community itself; there was a large measure of economic freedom, and but for this, it would hardly have been possible for the political life of Athens to develop as it did.

Capitalists and Contractors.

We have already seen that as early as the sixth century B.C. there was a class of wealthy capitalists, whose operations proved injurious to the cultivating peasantry. There is ample evidence of the importance of this class in connection with other sides of economic life. Private capital, with all the facilities it affords for enterprise both in industry and commerce, was being employed in every direction.

At first sight it might seem as if the field for private enterprise was rather limited, since the collectivist ideal of state-ownership was realised in Athens to a considerable extent;

[1] Ashley, *Econ. Hist.* I. ii. 33.

the State was the proprietor of the land, the mines, the harbours, and most of the means of production. Still the actual conduct of business was closely parallel to that with which we are familiar, since all public undertakings were let out on stated payments for longer or shorter periods to capitalists, who worked them for the time to their own advantage. Thus, though the resources of production were not appropriated by private persons, they were regularly administered by private capitalists who farmed them out. There was very little public administration, and what there was, was hopelessly corrupt.

The corruption among such public officials as did exist, was appalling; it brings to mind the stories of the maladministration in China, which were current during the late war. We can easily understand that in such a state of public morality, statesmen would be unwilling to extend the sphere of state operations. Xenophon indeed did suggest that the silver mines should be worked by the State for its own profit, instead of being farmed to contractors; but it does not appear that the proposal was ever carried out[1]. The fact that a proposal in favour of the administration of all material resources by government officials is seriously made in the present day, is a curious proof of the extraordinary growth of public morality and the increased confidence in its existence, in modern, as compared with ancient times. It corresponds with that other difference between the constructors of Utopias in ancient and modern times,—the former were unable to conceive the abolition of war, while the latter seem to think it unnecessary to take the possibility of war into account.

Some of the operations which were thus carried on by private capital were so large that no individual could undertake

---

[1] Xenophon's idea was that the State should turn capitalist, buy up slaves and let them out to contractors under state superintendents: the number of state-slaves could be increased with part of the profits so obtained, until with 10,000 a yearly income of 100 talents would accrue to the State. Xen. *De Vect.* ch. IV. 13 et seq.

them, and they were let to partnerships or associations of moneyed men. Such were the companies which undertook the farming of the various taxes. The collection of the harbour dues and the customs on imports, as well as the taxes on resident aliens, were all leased in this fashion. There might be agreements among wealthy men at the auctions to refrain from bidding, so that some tax might be let on easy terms[1], and there might be much oppression and extortion in the collection of revenue, but at all events the State obtained the command of a substantial sum. It is the simplest method of arranging for the collection of money-revenue, and it has been adopted in many lands, with similar convenience to the State, and similar oppression of the tax-payers.

The leases of the mines were made in perpetuity at a fixed sum, an exceptional arrangement, the grounds of which it is not quite easy to understand ; but the rest of the State property was leased for periods of years. The regulations which were made to bind the outgoing tenant as to cultivation, in the interest of his successors, are very instructive. Ten years appears to have been a usual term for the tenure of an estate[2], though land was also let for shorter periods.

Besides these undertakings[3] in connection with public property and public administration, there were other fields for the operations of private capitalists. The most honourable

---

[1] Alcibiades availed himself of the auction of the public revenues to extort a talent for a humble friend, by authorising him to bid a talent more than the previous farmers, who paid the difference to save their gains. Plut. *Alc.* v.   [2] Cf. Boeckh, II. 12, 16.

[3] The principle of joint stock association seems to have been well understood among the Greeks ; there was not the same scope for applying it on a large scale, as was afterwards offered at Rome ; it is chiefly mentioned in connection with shipowning, and commercial undertakings. Brant, *Les sociétés commerciales à Athènes* in *Revue de l'instruction publique en Belgique* (Gand, 1882), XXV. 113. There were also mining companies, companies for farming the revenue, and banking companies. M. de Kutorga, *Essai historique sur les trapézites ou banquiers d'Athènes,* read before the Acad. des Sci. Mor. et Pol. 24 Sept. 1859, p. 17.

employment was that of the spirited agriculturist, who bought land and worked and improved it, till the estate was in good cultivation and could be sold at a profit[1]. Other men might engage in merchandise, by personally travelling into foreign parts, or they could obtain a share in the profits of commercial ventures by lending money on "bottomry[2]". These opportunities for remunerative investment could be utilised not only by private persons, but as a means of obtaining a return on trust funds. The moneys of orphans appear to have been managed for them by the State; this was only natural, since the State also undertook the duty of supporting and educating cripples and the orphans of citizens, who had made no provision for their families[3]. Funds for the maintenance of orphans were also a recognised institution in the Roman Empire and in mediaeval times; the management of a similar trust continued to be a civic duty in London till after the time of the Great Fire. On the other hand we gather that the public treasure, which was amassed for a time to meet emergencies, was never utilised or invested in any way; it appears to have lain idle. There can be little doubt that Athens enjoyed an abundance of capital; in every department of life the intervention of capital and the presence of moneyed men eager for a profit, are obvious. Natural economy still reigned in households and on private estates; but money and capital were required in all paths of commercial enterprise and in carrying on the business of the State.

38. It has been pointed out above that money economy had been so far introduced in Athens as to affect the relations between employers and employed.

The organization of labour.

A great part of the labouring population of Athens consisted of wage-earners who had attained economic

---

[1] Xen. *Oec.* xx.

[2] I.e. on the security of a given vessel or cargo, for the voyage out or back or both.

[3] Boeckh, I. 323.

freedom. Some were citizens, who had political privileges, and others were resident aliens. It would be a mistake, however, to suppose that, because there was so much scope for the employment of free labour, slavery was either limited or exceptional. There was a sufficient number of free labourers to affect the political life of the city strongly[1], but there was in addition a large number of labourers who were not in any sense free economically, and still less politically[2].

The slaves were for the most part found in rural districts, though a certain amount of free labour found employment on the lands[3]; still the estates of the Athenian gentry were for the most part cultivated by slave labour. These men appear to have enjoyed a fairly comfortable lot; the rule of the better

[1] The great works undertaken by Pericles were chiefly carried out by wage-earners, i.e. by free labourers, either citizens or resident aliens. This is shown both by the direct statement of Plutarch (*Pericles* 12) and by the accounts which have been preserved (*Corp. Inscrip. Attic.* I. 321, 324). Meyer points out (*Wirthschaftliche Entwickelung*, 36) that there is scattered literary evidence, e.g. in Aristophanes, which goes to confirm this view as to a large class of free artisans. Compare also the excellent chapter "Du travail libre en Grèce" in Wallon, *Esclavage*, I.

[2] The figures of the population of Attica as given by Athenaeus (VI. 272) are 21,000 citizens, 10,000 metics, and 400,000 slaves, in 309 B.C. at the census taken by Demetrius of Phaleron. The figures for the citizens and metics at that date are highly probable, but Hume's suggestion (*Populousness of Ancient Nations* in *Essays*, I. 443) that 40,000 was the real number of slaves is rendered highly probable by the careful argument of Beloch (*Die Bevölkerung*, I. 95). On the other hand Wallon (*Esclavage*, I. 253) gives 40,000 as the probable figure for domestic slaves only, and places the total number at 201,000, or half the figure quoted from Athenaeus. Boeckh (*Pol. Ec. of Athens*, I. 52) adopts the larger estimate, and has worked out estimates of the town and country population and proportion of citizens and slaves, which have been generally adopted. Richter also argues (*Sklaverei*, 95) that Wallon has underestimated the probable numbers, and like Buchsenschütz (*Besitz und Erwerb*, 140) supports the credibility of the traditional figure of 400,000. But they wrote before Beloch had published his exhaustive discussion on the whole of this much disputed topic.

[3] Buchsenschütz, *op. cit.* 297.

masters was not oppressive[1]. But those who were condemned
to labour in the mines were, in all probability, treated with
much less consideration. Nor were the slaves who worked
as artisans in the factories of Athens in an enviable position;
they were at the mercy of capitalist speculators who had no
special interest in their welfare. Taken altogether the number
of slaves was very large; it was maintained by importation,
chiefly from the shores of the Black Sea, though piracy contributed its quota, prisoners taken in war, and citizens who had
fallen into poverty or crime might all be reduced to this
unenviable condition. There was no Greek who was free from
the shadow of possible slavery as a fate he might incur without
fault of his own.

Still from its earliest constitution, there had been a considerable number of resident aliens who worked at Athens for
wages, and steps were deliberately taken by Solon[2] to attract
them in greater numbers. There was also, especially in the
later periods, a large and ever increasing class of landless citizens
who were practically forced to maintain themselves by manual
occupation. In Athens itself it is probable that about half the
labouring population consisted of wage-earners.

It is clear that some of the public works at Athens were
carried on by means of hired labour; thus we hear of the
treasurer of the ship-builders and the treasurer of the builders
of the walls. But in many trades it is probable that a domestic
system prevailed and that a large amount of the industrial
activity at Athens was carried on by workmen in their own
shops and houses. For great operations, like the building of
a ship or a wall, the organisation of a number of labourers
was necessary, but ordinary commodities of every sort were
manufactured at home by workmen, each of whom had direct
dealings with customers.

It would be interesting if we knew how far these free or
alien craftsmen exercised a right to combine, such as was

[1] Xenophon, *Oec.* V. VII. IX. XII. XIII. XXI.   [2] Plutarch, *Solon*, 22, 24.

granted in many mediaeval cities to craft-gilds, which exercised
an exclusive authority over some given trade within the walls.
That Greek craftsmen like other craftsmen, had associations
and that they had common meals and common worship we
can hardly doubt[1]; it may certainly be questioned, however,
whether any such association attained to the status of a *corps-
de-métier* or craft-gild, and had the authoritative supervision of
a branch of trade, with the power of enforcing its decisions;
there is no evidence that such authoritative craft-gilds existed
at Athens in the time of Pericles.   The tone of Greek life was
against giving self-regulative powers to any group of artisans
and thus removing them and the disputes which might arise
in connection with their proceedings from the cognisance of
the general body of citizens.

Even though such workmen's associations as may have
existed in Greece were very different in character and powers
from their mediaeval analogues, it is not impossible that they
were the remote ancestors of the later institutions; in the
eranos there was a germ which would readily develop into a
true craft-gild so soon as appropriate circumstances offered;
the desire to get the full good of special skill, to preserve trade
secrets[2] and to prevent the intrusion of the incompetent would
operate among many artizans; some group of the resident
aliens might try to make special terms and to obtain special
trade privileges in connection with the payment of the tax to
which they were subjected[3].   The germs of trade organisations

---

[1] On the associations of different sorts which existed in Athens see
Beauchet, *Droit privé*, IV. 354.   The συνεργασία of wool-carders of Ephesus
is the only specific instance of an artizan association I have seen noted in a
Greek town, and even the evidence regarding that comes from the second
century A.D. (Wood, *Discoveries at Ephesus*, app. viii. no. 4).   The organisation of labour for getting in the harvest, referred to in Demosthenes, *C.
Nicostrat.* 21 (1253), seems rather to be a case of a contractor's gang than
a self-regulating association.

[2] Xenophon, *Oec.* XV.

[3] The Hanse merchants who were resident aliens in London held their

were there, and we cannot be surprised that associations of
this kind had been widely disseminated throughout the cities
of the Roman world at the time of the Christian era, and were
practically legitimatised by Alexander Severus.

39.   Money economy had not wholly displaced natural
economy in industry—wage-earners and slaves
worked side by side. The same holds good in
regard to the expenses of the State; the citizens
contributed their quota chiefly in the personal performance of
public duties, but there was also a considerable amount of
money which was raised by means of taxation.

Public Service and Taxation.

The public expenditure at Athens during the Persian War
and in the age of Pericles was very large; it is important to
see how this outlay was met. It may be well to point out,
however, that it is difficult to discern any distinct financial
principles underlying the scheme, which was wholly oppor-
tunist[1]. After the time of Solon the Athenians hardly used
the machinery of taxation to promote definite lines of national
development, whether agricultural or industrial.

Nor do great statesmen seem to have had any very definite views as to the best sources from which money could be
drawn, or as to the relative advantages of direct or indirect
taxation. As all the taxes were farmed, lump sums were paid
to the State, and the superior convenience or expensiveness of

privileges there on condition of repairing Bishopsgate. The craft-gilds in
Baroda and Ahmedabad appear to be organised in connection with the
collection of taxation.

[1] Pericles seems to have informed the Athenians that they need give
the allies no account of the tribute received, and he went on to assert "that
as the State was provided with all the necessaries of war, its superfluous
wealth should be laid out on such works as, when executed, would be
eternal monuments of its glory, and which during their execution, would
diffuse a universal plenty, for as so many kinds of labour and such a variety
of instruments and materials were requisite, to these undertakings every
art would be exerted, every hand employed, almost the whole city would
be in pay, and be at the same time both adorned and supported by itself."
Plutarch, *Per.* 12 (Langhorne's trans.).

different kinds of payment did not appear. The one broad principle of ancient finance was that the citizen should be free from such burdens as poll and land taxes, and should personally superintend the outlay of any sum he was called on to contribute, while other payments should be drawn from the non-free classes ; this principle was set aside in times of national disaster by the property tax.

There was much service that was rendered by citizens out of their private means, and to this extent the public purse was spared. The ordinary "liturgies," as they were called, recurred regularly ; such were the providing of a chorus, and the managing of the public games. The extraordinary liturgies, such as the trierarchy or fitting out a ship of war for a definite period, occurred at special times. The poorer citizens were exempt from undertaking duties of this kind ; while among the wealthy, there was a wholesome competition in the effort to discharge the public duties they undertook in a creditable fashion. This method of meeting the requirements of the State had many advantages, as the public demands were practically graduated according to the income of the citizens, while the ambition of the wealthy for distinction was turned to good account in the service of the State. Still, the system seems to have added seriously to the difficulties which arose from the short-sightedness of democracies[2]; it entailed a lack of permanent organisation which was most seriously felt in time of war, as it was difficult to bring the requisite pressure to bear so as to have a fund ready by a given date.

It is worth while to point out that this principle of relying on personal service for public duties, is familiar enough in later times, both for national and municipal affairs. The defence of England was an obligation which came upon all landowners even in pre-Norman times, and much of the police duty of

---

[1] Thucydides, VI. 54. 4. Boeckh, *Public Economy*, II. 42; see also Grote, IV. 145.

[2] Cunningham, *Modern Civilisation*, 182.

mediaeval cities rested with householders, who kept watch and ward. The navy, which met the Armada, was mostly equipped by private individuals out of public spirit; and at earlier times it had been the duty of towns to provide ships for national defence,—a claim which Charles I attempted to revive when he levied ship-money. Even the *choregia* has its analogy in the mistery plays or pageants, which were supported by different gilds of citizens in the Middle Ages: some existed for the object of providing a play, while other gilds, which had trade functions, devoted much of their wealth to pageants. Some of these contributions arose from the convenience of payment in kind or in service, rather than in money; but the system may have continued after money economy had completely superseded natural economy in finance, as a method of graduating the burdens which fell on the rich and poor respectively; it also combined the advantages of appealing to the public spirit of the rich and of bringing the necessary pressure to bear on those from whom a smaller outlay was expected.

Apart from these claims on the devotion of the citizens, there were various sources from which wealth could be obtained for public purposes. The principal resource on which the city-state could count, was its own property; in the case of Athens this consisted of lands, of valuable mines, and of harbours and remunerative public works. These, if wisely administered, might have continued to maintain the necessary expenses of state, at all events in time of peace. Once again, we have an analogy with English affairs; for, till the seventeenth century, it was generally assumed that the King should live of his own, though he might need aids from time to time and on special occasions; and many towns held considerable areas of land, the rents of which were applied to the common good.

(*a*) The chief economic difference between a town with a free constitution and one which was under the dominion of a tyrant or a military empire, lay in the fact that the town land, including the area on which the city stood, belonged in the one case to the citizens themselves, and in the other to the tyrant or conqueror as proprietor. Thus in the time of Pisistratus, a payment from the produce of their lands was demanded from citizens, as well as others, and under his successors the demand was continued at the rate of five per cent. When the Greek cities lost their freedom they became subject to similar obligations; but in their best days there was nothing analogous to a house-tax[1], any more than there was ordinarily a poll-tax for the free citizen. The land, as well as any houses belonging to the State, was let on lease, and the right of collecting the rents was farmed out by public auction.

(*b*) By far the most valuable property belonging to the Athenian State were the silver mines at Laurium. Silver requires a high degree of metallurgical knowledge to work, and it generally comes into use at a far later date than gold or copper; in the Homeric period it was little known in Greece, although such large supplies were subsequently obtained. The treasure procured from Laurium was invaluable to the Athenians during the Persian Wars; but the supply was, of course, not inexhaustible, though Xenophon seems to have regarded it as such[2]. He also fell into the curious mistake of believing that the value of silver would never fall, however much of it was put on the market, though he was aware that gold varied in value, like other commodities, according as much or little of it was available[3]. He argued accordingly that by working the silver mines energetically the Athenians might obtain annually a mass of treasure, which would be a more certain source of wealth, both in peace and war, than tribute from allies.

[1] The cities of England all grew up under royal, ecclesiastical, or baronial protection, and were subject to payments to their superiors, which they generally raised by means of a house-rate assessed among themselves.
[2] See Xen. *De Vect.* IV.
[3] *Ib.* IV. He admitted that plenty of gold always lowered its value, and raised the price of silver, but held that silver could never lose its value.

(*c*) The theatres and the harbours were, in a way, remunerative public works. The former came soon to be a cause of public pauperisation, as the price of a seat was distributed to the citizens; and the State thus gave a subvention which must have absorbed most of, and perhaps more than all the rental received. In the case of the harbours there were no similar outgoings, and the dues were paid by all vessels using them; while there seem to have been similar charges made for permission to store goods or corn in the public warehouses and granaries. These were the chief works of a remunerative character which had been erected at Athens at public expense.

(*d*) The State also obtained a considerable revenue from its judicial functions; the administration of justice was not merely self-supporting, but actually profitable. The Athenians were eminently litigious, and the fees in civil actions came to a large sum; while the fines in criminal cases, not to mention the confiscations in political trials, went into the public treasury. By assuming a sovereignty over the allies, Athens secured a considerable judicial revenue in addition to the tribute. Appeals, at all events, if not small cases, had to be decided at Athens; and the fees, together with the outlay of the suitors and the witnesses, formed an important source of revenue to the State, and of profit to the inhabitants. In this aspect we may compare the large pecuniary remittances which were made to the Court of Rome in the Middle Ages in connection with legal proceedings; but it has been a common practice at many times to treat jurisdiction as a source of revenue. The profit which arose from the jurisdiction over a given area of England at the time of the Norman Conquest was very considerable. The Abbey at Ely was a large ecclesiastical community which had comparatively little land, but was amply endowed with judicial rights, as the soke or rights of jurisdiction extended over a large area.

(*e*) The tribute from the allies was the largest portion of the Athenian revenue, and, as events proved, the least secure.

The circumstances under which it arose, and the subsequent history, the commutation of exactions for money payments, and the transference of the treasure to Attic soil, under the pretence of protecting it more securely, are well-known facts; and their grave influence on the destinies of Athens need not be pointed out. There is no special economic significance in the exacting of tribute, which was the most obvious of all ways of using power as a source of revenue; and it was the familiar expedient of Eastern kings. There was possibly some ingenuity in exacting it as a tribute not from conquered peoples, but from friendly allies; but it is an expedient on which it is unnecessary to dwell.

(*f*) There are some difficulties in regard to the tax on resident aliens and the question how far it was levied from all, how far commutation was possible, and so forth, but the broad mark of discrimination which it drew between the citizen and the alien is clear enough. In mediaeval times, this distinction was rigidly adhered to; the kings of England exacted heavier duties from aliens than from denizens, while all municipal finance drew a distinction between the burgesses who were at 'scot and lot'[1] and paid their rates, and the men who were foreign to the town[2]; these latter were only allowed to enjoy its privileges as a centre for trade by paying tolls, or by compounding for freedom from tolls in a regular payment to the town.

(*g*) The customs on exports and imports were also a source of substantial revenue; we gather from Xenophon that the import duty on slaves alone was a considerable sum. Had the Athenians endeavoured to make the most of their magnificent commercial position, they might have developed a very considerable trade; but while they positively discouraged a carrying trade, they were at no pains to develop native

---

[1] Gross, *Gild Merchant*, I. 53.

[2] Boeckh, *Public Economy*, II. 49. For mediaeval analogies compare Cunningham, *Alien Immigrants*, 40, 92.

industries which should supply them with products as well as manufactures to export.

Besides these customs duties at the port, there were also *octroi* duties at the city gates on goods coming to market. The richer citizens, who had their own means of support in their own estates, probably escaped from these taxes, but they would form an indirect burden on the poorer citizens, and would also press on the much enduring aliens.

(*h*) These may all be regarded as ordinary sources of revenue. In extraordinary emergencies a direct tax was levied on the property of all who were living under the protection of the State. It seems at first sight singular that self-taxation should have been so readily voted as appears to have been done by so great a body of citizens, though the large crowd of paupers would have little to pay, and might indeed have a sweet pleasure in imposing a burden on more fortunate neighbours. The internal balance of wealth differed from the internal balance of power in the State.

These different branches of Athenian finance are of considerable interest, for they give us precedents for almost all the expedients that have been since adopted, in commercial countries and cities, for raising money by taxation. The modern analogies in regard to unpaid service and to property have been already noted; the various kinds of taxes have their correlatives also. It is necessary to remember, too, that Athens was a state as well as a city, and that she furnishes precedents in regard to national as well as municipal finance.

The property tax was purely political, and it has its analogue in the ecclesiastical tithe, as well as in the taxes on moveables which were introduced in England under Henry II and eventually took shape as tenths and fifteenths. But the other kinds of taxation are two-sided, partly political and partly municipal. Some of the taxes corresponded to our national revenue as it was in the Middle Ages; a portion of the judicial revenue was analogous to the income arising from the pleas

of the Crown, while the extra alien customs and payments from
aliens for chartered privileges, as well as the customs, were
similar in both cases.   On the other hand the municipal side
of Athenian finance is reflected in the mediaeval payments of
retailers[1] and others who were 'foreign' to the mediaeval towns,
and of octroi duties; these later municipal authorities had also
some local jurisdiction, such as the assize of bread and ale,
which was by no means unremunerative.

40.   With such resources at command the Athenians might
have built up a city which should enjoy a long   Pericles and
era of commercial prosperity; an example of   Unproductive
this kind had already been set by Miletus and   Public Works.
by Tyre.   These cities had consciously endeavoured to establish a successful manufacturing community at home[2]; but the
Athenians cherished no such desire.   As a state their selfish
ambition undermined the sources of their wealth and power;
and as a city their skill and treasure were lavished by Pericles
on unproductive public works.

With the policy of expending so much treasure[3] in great
public works we are not concerned; Pericles appears to have
believed that the course he pursued added to the prestige
of Athens, while it certainly put money in circulation and gave
employment and occupation to the citizens.   Whether he was
right in his calculations or not we need not discuss; his critics
held that his efforts to raise the prestige of Athens only served
to rouse the jealousy of her allies[4].   It may be doubted
whether Athens could under any circumstances have retained
her political supremacy; when the Persians were defeated, the
common fear which held the allies together was set at rest,
and the political system of which Athens was the centre lost

---

[1] Hibbert, *Gilds*, 148.

[2] But Miletus appears to have continued to trade in raw wool as well.
Grothe, *op. cit.* 282.

[3] For calculations as to the actual cost see Leake, *Topography*, I. 461.

[4] Plutarch, *Pericles*, 12.

its cohesion. We may be satisfied to look at Athens, not as a political power, but as an 'economic' city, a centre of active industry and enterprising commerce. The lines on which the energies and enterprise of the citizens were directed by Pericles were not those which favoured the permanent prosperity of the industrial and commercial life of the city[1].

The economic results of his undertakings can be more clearly seen when we contrast the aims of Pericles with those which were deliberately pursued by the Phoenicians. The slave labour imported into Tyre and the materials obtained were turned to account in manufactures, which could be sold to other countries and thus create a source of wealth; this gave the means of procuring more materials and more labour for the renewal and increase of industry, and thus afforded opportunities for farther progress in wealth. On the other hand the works of Pericles served no economic purpose but that of display; they could not be realised in money, or exported to other lands, or utilised for the production of more wealth. The skill and treasure devoted to them were permanently sunk; their construction afforded a means of employing the people; but, when completed, they provided no employment for industry and no incentive to trade. When large sums are laid out in productive public works like those of the Egyptians at Lake Moeris, wealth so expended not only gives employment at the time, but affords facilities for continued employment afterwards. Harbours, canals, irrigation, roads, railways or anything else that opens up a country may have this character. Pericles, in endeavouring to find profitable employment for the people, deliberately turned their energies to unproductive public works; the magnificent buildings which were reared

---

[1] Even if he was right in his political view and the buildings did promote the prestige of Athens, this did not necessarily bring in solid material advantages. Capital may be sunk in procuring political status without an adequate pecuniary return. The proceedings of the two English East India Companies may be instanced as cases in point.

under his direction absorbed the wealth of the city, without developing any natural resources or trading facilities in return. The treasure was exhausted once for all, and there was no means of replacing it, such as arises with capital employed in industry or trade; it was locked up in forms that are artistically superb, but economically worthless.

There may be sentimentalists who are shocked at any such philistine efforts to appraise the economic importance of the grandest works of architectural art. But after all we may appreciate them better if we know what they cost; we may still feel that they were well worth the cost, but at least let us recognise what it was. A heroic action may cost a man his life, and we may hold it was a deed that was well worth dying for. So too it may be that the buildings on the Acropolis were well worth the strain they caused; it is none the less true that they helped to exhaust the energies of Athens. The sinking of capital in works that are ultimately productive may cause temporary disaster, as in the Railway mania of the present century; but the economic effect of raising and maintaining the great buildings at Athens was more serious[1]. They proved to be a mere drain on the accumulated wealth of the present, while they gave no help of any sort for producing more wealth in the future[2]. The wealth of Miletus was continually circulating, and gave the means for an industrial community to grow and flourish; the wealth of Athens and her allies was sunk, once for all, in creations of marvellous beauty.

41. The achievements, which are among the greatest glories of Athens, were thus one of the causes of its decline. At the same time it is probable that even if her treasures had been better employed, and the commerce and industry of Athens

[1] On the degeneracy of Athens and inability to recover after the ravages committed by Philip in 200 B.C. compare Finlay, *History of Greece*, I. 55.

[2] On the disastrous effects, under the Roman Empire, of the sinking of capital, together with the failure to replace it from other sources, see below, p. 184.

had been developed, she could scarcely have succeeded in
the struggle to avert conquest; the cities which
used their wealth most wisely did not maintain
their power. Tyre and Miletus failed to resist
the onslaught of the Persians, and it is difficult
to believe that Athens could have attained, in
any circumstances, to such naval and military power as to
preserve her freedom in the political conditions of the times.
Still it is worth while to look closely at the economic causes
which co-operated to weaken her, and rendered her decline in
wealth and power more certain and rapid than would otherwise have been the case.

Economic
causes of the
decline in the
material
prosperity
of Athens.

So far as the property of Athens was concerned, there was
much short-sightedness in the manner of its consumption. It
is possible to till the surface of the earth so that it shall
be steadily and continuously productive; but when minerals
are taken from a quarry or mine, the supply is necessarily
decreased. Exhaustion must occur sooner or later. This is so
palpable that it is difficult to understand how Xenophon should
have questioned it, or the Greek statesmen should have drawn
so recklessly on these resources. But it is at least a warning
to any country, the pre-eminence of which rests in some degree
on mineral wealth. The Athenian democracy continued to
believe that their silver was inexhaustible, until it was worked
out; and in much the same way it is difficult to get the English
public to believe that the coal seams cannot continue to be
worked at a profit in the future for an unassignable length of
time.

But a more obvious reason of failure lay in the economic
misuse of capital, which was employed for the erection of unproductive and not of remunerative public works. It might
have been used to improve agriculture, to foster some kind of
manufacturing, or to develop commerce. In such cases it
would have helped to organise a regular department of economic life, and wealth could have been produced steadily

and continuously. But industry was not directed into these channels; it was devoted instead to works of magnificence and display, which testified to great attainments, but could not be used so as to promote subsequent progress.

Further than this, there was a good deal of expenditure which did not promote the prosperity of the State in any way. The payments to the poorer citizens for their judicial duties, and for their seats in the theatre, were at best a waste of public money; while they opened the way for corrupt judgments and they also tended to the pauperisation of the citizens. It was useless to enjoin labour on the one hand, and on the other to supply political payments which helped the less reputable citizens to subsist without labour. On every side it may be said that Athenian finance was extravagant and wasteful; the mineral resources were recklessly worked, the capital was mis-directed and the citizens were pauperised.

CHAPTER III.

ALEXANDER'S EMPIRE AND THE HELLENISTIC
PERIOD.

42. In the preceding sections we have traced the development of Greek civilization on Greek soil; we must now turn to consider its diffusion over a large area of the world. In a way, history repeated itself. It has been pointed out above how the successful invasion of the Hyksos directed the attention of the Pharaohs towards the East and eventually brought about a war of revenge and the formation of a great Egyptian empire; so the invasions of the Persians and their failure incited Alexander to pursue a career of conquest; the war of retaliation led eventually to permanent expansion[1]. Even the results which were immediately attained had far-reaching effect; for Alexander came so near to realising his ambition of forming a universal Empire, that his success gave colour to the dreams of conquest which have floated before other men, such as Pyrrhus or Caesar or Napoleon. But he did far more than this; for though his career was brief, he not only set the example of successful conquest, but he also indicated the manner in which a huge empire might be rendered a civilizing agency, as well as a military organisation. It is unnecessary to suppose, as some panegyrists seem to do, that he had much

Alexander's Conquests and Aims.

[1] Alexander's work did for his era what the Crusades effected for the Germanic peoples; both movements opened up new spheres of activity and brought about the development of a new culture. Richter, *Handel und Verkehr*, p. 116.

missionary enthusiasm for diffusing Greek culture throughout the world. He was a 'tyrant[1]' rather than an exponent of the best developments of Greek polity; his conquests raised the prestige[2] of Greece among the barbarians, but as a statesman, he was so far from treating the distinction between Greek and barbarian as fundamental[3], that he aimed at a fusion of the Greek and Oriental worlds. He adopted eastern manners[4], he encouraged the intermarriage of the two races[5], and he planned a policy of effecting compulsory migrations[6] and transplantations of conquered peoples, which had been practised by the Assyrians, and was subsequently carried out by the Romans; the severance of territorial attachments might render the people more subservient to imperial rule and more easily organised for military purposes. Under his rule, and that of his successors, the Greek ideals were to some extent degraded by contact with the East[7]; but in his efforts to found a permanent military empire, Alexander seems to have perceived the importance of commerce[8] as a source of wealth and power; he secured his hold upon the conquered territory by the settlement and development of new cities[9], and for these undertakings he drew on the industrial and commercial experience of Greece.

[1] Holm, *History of Greece*, III. 354. [2] *Ib.* III. 289.
[3] *Ib.* III. 385. [4] *Ib.* III. 348, 386
[5] *Ib.* III. 360. [6] Grote, XII. 356.

[7] "He might also have reflected that two races of different civilization cannot be blended by degrading the higher and more independent one to the level of the other and depriving it of the privileges to which it is accustomed." Holm, III. 355.

[8] The bringing of the hoards of the Persian Empire into circulation gave a fresh impetus to trade. The Graeco-Macedonian development of the court put a stop to the Persian payments in kind, and acted as a direct encouragement to interchange of Oriental affluence and Occidental arts, and set a high standard of luxurious life among the rich. Richter, *Handel und Verkehr*, p. 112.

[9] "In founding so many cities he recognised the autonomous Greek city-community as the basis of his empire" (Holm, III. 386); it contrasted with the village life of the East. Mitteis, *Reichsrecht u. Volksrecht*, 20.

The Persian empire was his model, but he improved upon the model by planting cities and fostering commerce. The Persian king, according to Xenophon, was devoted to two arts, war and husbandry[1]; and these were the mainstay of the empire. Alexander, with his knowledge of the strength of Tyre, Rhodes and other commercial cities, was fully alive to the importance of organising similar centres of trade. It is true that of the seventy cities which he is said to have planted, many were military stations and fortified camps; but for Alexandria, at all events, a site was chosen which was admirably adapted for commerce; while the project of founding a commercial emporium at the mouth of the Euphrates shows that Alexander could utilise commercial opportunities[2]. It is difficult to believe too, that the expeditions which he organised for circumnavigating Arabia, and for the contemplated exploration of the Caspian, were merely intended to discover new worlds to conquer. They are far more intelligible if we regard them as exploring expeditions, which were at least partly undertaken with the object of opening up trade; and this interpretation is fully borne out by the interest Alexander displayed in commerce[3]. He did not live long enough to give effect to his

[1] Xen. *Oec.* IV.

[2] Grote, X. 189, 190.

[3] We may compare his scheme for uniting the Black Sea and Caspian by means of a canal. Droysen, *Hellenismus*, III. ii. 177. He had the interests of commerce at heart in the positions he chose for some of his cities, though others were primarily forts (Thirlwall, *History*, VII. 120). Of Alexander's work, as a whole, from an economic aspect, Thirlwall says (*Ib.* 121): "Let any one endeavour to enter into the feelings with which a Phoenician merchant must have viewed the change that took place in the face of the earth, when the Egyptian Alexandria had begun to receive and pour out an inexhaustible tide of wealth: when Babylon had become a great port: when a passage was opened both by sea and land between the Euphrates and the Indus: when the forests on the shores of the Caspian had begun to resound with the axe and the hammer. It will then appear that this part of the benefits which flowed from Alexander's conquest cannot be easily exaggerated."

schemes for organising and administering the vast territory he
had conquered; that work was chiefly done by his generals
after his death; but there is sufficient indication to shew that
he recognised its importance, with reference to his great
designs. He was aware that a military empire must have a
well-administered military system, and that resources can be
obtained not only from careful husbandry but by promoting
industry and trade.

43. Philip of Macedon had prepared the means by
which his son conquered so triumphantly[1].   Greek
Alexander had excellent soldiers at his com-   Officials.
mand, for the Macedonian army had been admirably drilled
and organised; but he was also well provided with the sinews
of war, for the whole resources of Macedonia had been
devoted to furnishing military equipment and supplies. The
army was the one department of public life on which money
was expended. It was possibly Alexander's intention to
organise the whole of his vast empire on the same model and
for the same purpose, and to establish arsenals like those of
Pella at many points. For this administrative work he could
rely on assistance from the Greeks, since their political and
business habits rendered them excellent officials; the immediate
result of the conquest was to open up an enormous field for
the activity of individual Greeks. The vast treasures of the
Persian empire served to stimulate their ambition and excite
their cupidity; while the financial business in connection with
such large revenues must have offered great opportunities to
Greek capitalists. The Persian administration had become
most chaotic[2]; it retained some elements of natural economy,

---

[1] " It is clearly established that Philip regarded his work in Greece as
completed, and was preparing to do what Alexander afterwards did."
Holm, III. 289.

[2] It is to be noticed however that the Persian administrative system as
introduced by Darius Hystaspis was a great improvement at the time. He
divided the whole empire into satrapies and fixed the tribute that was to be

so that financial checks and counter-checks hardly existed[1]; and the inspectors, who were sent round at intervals, exercised no effective control over the satraps; Greek officials were able to introduce better methods of administration[2]. But it is in connection with Egypt that we have the fullest information in regard to the system of government at this period. Recent discoveries have thrown fresh, if imperfect, light on the fiscal system of Egypt under the Ptolemies, and help us to see how skilfully the government was organised under these monarchs, so as to relieve the peasantry from the exactions in forced labour and in produce which had oppressed them in byegone days. A papyrus discovered by Mr Flinders Petrie gives us an immense amount of information on the collection of revenue under Ptolemy Philadelphus in Egypt. The whole presents a glimpse of an interesting state of transition between a natural and a money economy. As money does not appear to have

paid from each. 'During all the reign of Cyrus and afterwards when Cambyses ruled, there were no fixed tributes, but the nations severally brought gifts to the king.' Herod. III. 89 (Rawlinson). Administrative changes, such as Darius introduced, are of supreme importance, in as much as they limit the opportunities for *arbitrary* extortion, and introduce the possibility of regularity and system in public finance; of course the system may be more *oppressive* than the laxity it supersedes. Corresponding changes may be noted in connection with the terms of land tenure in England—uncertain fines—regular rents paid in kind or service—money rents.

[1] For alleged attempts to maintain control by playing off one official against another, see Xenophon, *Cyro.* VIII. vi. 3; *Oec.* iv.; also the essay on *Persian Administration* in Rawlinson's *Herod.* III. 358, and *Ancient Monarchies*, IV. 425.

[2] Alexander must have had the permanent administration of his conquests in mind, when he first came to Asia for the arrangements which he made in Sardis after the victory at the Granicus were governed by the same principles which he always followed afterwards....Alexander's system protected both government and people better than the Persian one. Alexander sometimes appointed natives as administrative officials (satraps) in the central and eastern provinces....Yet we note that when a change was necessary Macedonians took the place of natives. Holm, III. 378.

been coined in ancient Egypt, this fiscal system may fairly be regarded as of later introduction, and may be ascribed with probability to the influence of the Greeks, who had elaborated it in connection with the revenues of cities; and, since the payment of taxes in kind was still maintained in a region like the Fayum which had been recently re-colonised, it probably had even a firmer hold in other parts of the Hellenistic world. The produce of the soil was treated in various ways. Oil was a state monopoly, of which the production and sale were carefully supervised[1]. The vineyards and orchards, on the other hand, were left under private management, and one-sixth of the produce was paid to the state; the owners of orchards assessed the value of their crops themselves[2]; if the tax-farmers agreed, this sum was accepted; but if the farmers valued the crop higher, they might seize it and sell it, and after paying the peasant the full sum at which he had valued his crop himself, they might keep any surplus; on the other hand, if they had over-estimated the value of the crop, they would have to pay the tax, or a portion of it, out of their own pockets[3]. It was on the whole a fair system of valuation, for the peasant was protected against extortion, while the tax-farmer was interested in seeing that enough was paid; when the tax was paid in money, it was collected by the oeconomus, a royal official[4], and the tax-farmers came in as speculators in raw produce; their intervention facilitated the collection of a money revenue without compelling the peasantry to pay in money. They were continually realising the produce and making payments,

---

[1] B. P. Grenfell, *Revenue Laws*, 47 f. It appears that the whole was organised with the view of providing a plentiful supply of oil, both for cooking and lighting at Alexandria.

[2] Grenfell, *Revenue Laws*, 29. These written documents embodying their self-assessment would serve as the basis for a regularly accepted census later.

[3] Grenfell, *Revenue Laws*, 29, 2–21, p. 101.

[4] *Ib.* p. 105.

C. W. C.

9

but the accounts were balanced once a month[1], while there was a general balancing at the end of the term for which the contractors had agreed[2]. It was a complicated system, but it permitted the constant readjustment of the amounts to be paid, as the crops varied; if the speculators contracted for a period of years, they took the risk of changing seasons alike off the hands of the peasantry and of the government. Of course, in cities, where money economy was in full vogue, this particular field for speculation was not open, though the collection of such taxation was also let by auction. The whole story of a later Joseph, and of the success with which he made his fortune, by outbidding a ring of capitalists, and then raising a revenue by shameless extortion, is not a little instructive[3]. It shows what opportunities there were for private gain, even in a well-organised empire. The modern stories of the pillaging of Begums and Rajahs by the East India Company's servants, or of the exploiting of the Roman Provinces under the Republic, give us some idea of the possibilities of plunder which lay open to Greek adventurers in connection with the administration of Alexander's empire, and the kingdoms into which it was divided.

44. It was thus that in the Hellenistic period the Greek genius was called on to take its part in the organisation of great empires; this was a new departure, and it was left for the Romans to carry out this work on a larger scale and more permanently. But there was also much to be done in planting, throughout the known world, centres of civilized society, similar to those which had played such an important part in the development of Greek culture. The city could no longer serve as a political ideal for men who had once been affected by cosmopolitan ambitions; distant conquest could not be

Greek Cities and Confederations. Rhodes.

---

[1] Grenfell, *Revenue Laws*, 16, p. 84.

[2] *Ib.* 18, 19, p. 88.

[3] Josephus, *Ant.* XII. 4. 4.

undertaken by citizen soldiers, nor could administration be wisely entrusted to men who had a sense of being expatriated and in exile[1]. Political and military duty abroad was incompatible with keen personal attachment to the life in one distinct city. The large city, which was necessary for military defence, might be too cumbrous to be a well-organised centre of civilised life[2]. The conception of a state was separating itself from that of a town ; but though bereft of its exclusive importance, city life still retained much of its value. Cities afforded the sphere where the arts of life and the culture, which the Greeks had attained, could be most easily maintained and perpetuated. By planting new cities on the old model[3], the Greeks succeeded in carrying their civilization with them and diffusing it throughout the world[4].

In this period we come across many instances of the later type of Greek city, which did not merely grow under favourable conditions, but which was deliberately planted[5]. The most celebrated example of a city, which was systematically laid out with two main streets and a large square for the transaction of business, was the Piraeus at Athens[6]. Hippodamus of Miletus was the architect who devised the plan, and at a subsequent date he was employed to lay out cities at

[1] This has proved a recurring difficulty in connection with French colonisation.

[2] Aristotle, *Politics*, VII. 4.

[3] Mitteis, *op. cit.* 78. On the affiliation of mediaeval burghs as a means of diffusing a body of custom, see Gross, *Gild Merchant*, I. 241.

[4] On the Greek colonies of this period see Droysen, *Die Städtegrund-ungen Alexanders und seiner Nachfolger*, in *Hellenismus*, III. ii. 189. It was an advantageous policy also because it relieved the pressure of population at home. Philip himself had contemplated settlements of needy Greeks in Asia after its conquest (Isocrates, V. 120), and the expansion of Macedon immediately relieved the Greek cities and islands of a disaffected multitude which had fostered civil war and piracy. Meyer, *Die wirth-schaftliche Entwickelung des Alterthums*, p. 41.

[5] See above, p. 96.

[6] Leake, *Topography*, I. 381, 383.

Thurii[1] and at Rhodes[2]. The older and newer methods of
building are contrasted by Aristotle[3] and by Pausanias[4]; and
the schemes of the newer builders not only provided for
public convenience and traffic, but assigned separate sites for
private houses. Deinocrates, the architect whom Alexander
employed, doubtless carried out this method of arrangement in
the cities which he laid out[5].

[1] Diod. Sic. XII. 10. The city of Thurii was divided across by four
broad streets and lengthwise by three.

[2] Strabo, XIV. 654; on the work of Hippodamus as an architect and
surveyor compare M. Erdmann's article in *Philologus*, XXII. 193.

[3] Aristotle, *Politics*, VII. 11. He had also opinions on the constitution
and organisation of a city. *Ib.* II. 5.

[4] On Elis, quoted by Leake, *op. cit.* 383 n.

[5] Richter, *Handel und Verkehr*, 117. The plans of Alexandria (Kiepert,
Zur Topographie des alten Alexandria nach Mahmud Beg's Entdeckungen,
1872) and of Antioch (K. O. Müller, *De Antiq. Antiochenae*) seem to show
that these towns were rectangular, and that main streets ran into the
corners of the market-place of its sides. The type is quite distinct from
that of the Roman towns, as described by the *agrimensores*, Lachmann,
Gromatici Veteres, I. 180, II. 339 ; it seems probable that in this matter the
Romans did not follow the Greek system as exemplified at Thurii (Diod.
Sic. XII. 10), but carried on the practice which they had apparently derived
from the Etruscans (Cantor, *Römische Agrimensoren*, 65). When there
was a revival of town life in the thirteenth century, and many towns were
laid out in the south of France, the plan which was adopted seems to
have been very similar to that which approved itself to the Greeks.
Montpazier is probably the best example (Verneilh, *Architecture Civile* in
Didron, *Annales Archéologiques*, VI. 73), but a similar arrangement was
adopted in several towns in Perigord, and is even found at Winchelsea and
Salisbury. The art of laying out cities, as practised by Maynard and other
mediaeval engineers may have been a new invention; but many peoples, as
e.g. in India, have never attempted anything of the kind, and it is unlikely
that this method was re-originated afresh, even though we have no means of
proving whence it was derived. At the same time it is to be noticed that in
the area in France where the towns of this type arose, there are very definite
traces of intercourse with the East and of the influence of Byzantine architecture; F. Verneilh, *Architecture Byzantine*, 125. It is by no means impossible that the idea of laying out a city on this regular plan was suggested
by what might be seen in Alexandria or Antioch, or some other commercial
centre.

Of the cities founded in this period the two most important were Alexandria and Antioch. The former under the wise rule of the Ptolemies soon attained to great magnificence as a commercial city. The rise of manufacturing and commercial towns on the Mediterranean had at length transformed Egypt into a commercial country; the corn trade became regularly organised and cargoes were sent not only to Attica, but to Puteoli for Italian consumption. When the country thus rose into commercial importance, it was easy to divert a portion of the stream of caravan traffic so as to pass down the Nile[1]; the products of India[2] and Arabia could thus be brought to Alexandria and exchanged for the silver, wine, amber and fabrics which came from the Mediterranean lands[3]. Roads were constructed across the desert from Berenice and Myoshormos to Coptos, and attempts were made to clear the Red Sea of Arabian pirates.

Antioch on the Orontes was even more favourably situated for caravan traffic from India by the Euphrates. Both these cities became centres of Greek learning and science as well as of commerce. The spirit of the age found expression in the edifices which were raised; the greatest building[4] of this

[1] Richter, *Handel und Verkehr*, 119.

[2] "Harpalos discovered or rediscovered the cause of the monsoons, and at the proper seasons Arabian fleets went to and fro between the Malabar coast and the harbours sedulously constructed by the Ptolemies on the Red Sea." Percy Gardner, *New Chapters in Greek History*, p. 437.

[3] Compare the account of the commercial advantages and trade of Alexandria given by Strabo (XVII. 798). It was "for ages the pivot of the Indian traffic." Poole, *Cities of Egypt*, p. 181. Special favour was extended to the Jews by the Ptolemies. At Alexandria they were placed on a level with the Greeks, above the native Egyptians. *Ib.* 186.

[4] In the public works and buildings of earlier Hellas, the useful was sacrificed to the ornamental: in the Hellenistic period the reverse was the case. As typical of this period may be taken the Pharos at Alexandria, the drainage of Lake Copais, the canal between the Red Sea and Nile. The Hellenistic monarchies had far larger revenues than the Hellenic cities, and used them better. Paparrigopoulo, *Civilization Hellénique*, pp. 92-94.

epoch seems to have been neither a palace nor a temple but
the Museum at Alexandria. It was an extraordinary foundation, in which the attempt was made to gather together all
literature, and all sorts of instruments of study; even though
subsequent changes have entirely destroyed all traces of it, we
ought to bear it in mind. It serves to show that in this age of
conquest the claims of learning and the duty of advancing
knowledge were not entirely overlooked[1], while the diffusion of
the Greek language afforded a medium through which they
could be readily communicated. The work done at Alexandria
in collecting and preserving the writings of older Greece was
as valuable as that of Constantinople in after ages.

These were but two out of innumerable foundations in
which the Greek type of city, as an economic and commercial
centre, was preserved[2]. They were not free cities, but had
to pay tribute; they had no political status in making peace
or war, but almost all of them had powers of internal self-
government[3]. All the sources of revenue and matters of jurisdiction and police which have been described in a foregoing
section as municipal might well be in their hands; the city, as
an economic unit and a centre of industrial and commercial life,
was able to fulfil its functions in much the same way whether it
was politically free or was embraced within the area and control of a military empire. The rise of the Macedonian power
had proved the impossibility of autonomous city life; when
the Greeks were once drawn into contact with the empires of
the East, no mere city could secure for itself the protection
from external attack which is necessary in order to render

[1] Mahaffy, *Empire of the Ptolemies*, p. 92 *et seq.*

[2] Under the Diadochi the number of these cities rose to at least two
hundred. Paparrigopoulo, *Civilization Hellénique*, p. 73.

[3] Alexandria was an exception in this matter. It was a royal residence,
and quite distinct from city foundations of the Graeco-Macedonian conquest
elsewhere. Even here however the inhabitants had privileges and status
which gave them relief from taxation and other advantages. Mahaffy,
Empire of the Ptolemies, pp. 76, 77.

economic progress possible. Some more extensive forms of
political organisation were necessary in the new circumstances,
and this seems to have been felt even by the cities which preserved their independence. The Greek cities of the Aegean
formed themselves into a federation of which Rhodes was the
leading spirit: for a time they were able to attain security for
their maritime trade, and to advance to an extraordinary
condition of prosperity[1]. The leading cities of a previous
generation had succumbed in the wars ; Miletus, Halicarnassus,
and Tyre had suffered from the Persians, and from Alexander
himself, and trade would easily revert to other centres[2]. The
Rhodians obtained the naval supremacy which Athens lost,
and they succeeded in gaining their ends in their commercial
rivalry with Egypt. The story of the earthquake which destroyed their city, and of the magnanimous efforts of other
towns to restore the harbour in all its magnificence[3], is often
spoken of as testifying to the unity of sentiment which prevailed throughout the Hellenistic world, despite the political
divisions and the competing military ambitions[4]; whatever

[1] The tendency towards federations in Greece proper is also seen in the
Achaean and Aetolian Leagues. Both Rhodes (Mahaffy, *Empire*, 62) and
the Achaean League owed much to Egyptian support. Ptolemy II. gave
Aratus twenty-five talents at one time, 150 at another, and Ptolemy III.
was appointed generalissimo (Mahaffy, *op. cit.* 190, 203). The members of
the League retained their political institutions, but laws, weights, measures,
money, magistrates, councillors, and judges were the same for all. Polybius, II. 37, 10.

[2] *e.g.* Corinth, Pergamus, Ephesus, and Smyrna rose into fresh importance as emporia.

[3] This comes out most clearly in the recognition of a common law
among the scattered Greek cities. Mitteis, *op. cit.* 62, 75.

[4] The siege of Rhodes, as well as the earthquake, reveals the general
anxiety of kingdoms and cities to preserve the integrity of the great trading
centres in the interests of Mediterranean commerce. Cf. Polybius, v. 88.
"The whole chapter indicates that the solvency of Rhodes implied the
solvency of all the neighbouring powers, and that bankruptcy there would
have produced a commercial crisis all over the civilised world." Mahaffy,
224–5, also 60, 61. Cf. Meyer, *op. cit.* p. 46.

truth there may be in this view, it is also clear that commercial interests required the maintenance of this commercial centre. By the federation of Rhodes two conditions were realised which are absolutely necessary for the healthy and continued life of commercial cities, and which none could hope to be strong enough to obtain for itself alone,—the establishment of a rule or "sovereignty" which afforded security for commercial intercommunication without attack from pirates, and the enforcement of good customs and laws among the traders from different centres. The earliest code of maritime law bears the name of Rhodes, and though many of the customs are doubtless older than this confederation, there were conditions for enforcing them regularly and over a large area under her leadership such as had hardly existed before[1].

45. By the growth of these military empires and political federations we see that the city life, which had flourished so greatly among the Greeks, had proved itself wanting. Just as in earlier times the household had ceased to be the type of political organisation, and had survived as an economic institution in that larger whole—the city, so now the city itself was superseded as the highest type of political life. The city survived too, but merely as an institution in military empires, not as the centre of the whole ; just because it ceased to have so much political significance we can see its economic importance more clearly. The attempt to found a Greek universal empire was short-lived, but the cities which had been planted as Greek colonies in the Mediterranean lands continued to be centres of industry and depots of commerce ; they had

Lasting Economic Importance of Greek Cities.

---

[1] The Rhodian Law *de jactu* was adopted into the civil law of Rome by Augustus. (*Digest*, XIV. tit. 2.) "It is supposed that the laws of Oleron, and indeed those of all maritime nations, are more or less remotely traceable to a Rhodian origin, if not indeed, to the still higher antiquity of the yet more ancient Phoenicians." Colquhoun, *Summary of the Roman Civil Law*, III. 137.

sufficient vitality to preserve and transmit the arts of peace through all the struggles for the empire of the world.

We have traced the general introduction of money economy among the Greeks and the consequent development of the city as a sphere for the activities of the free citizens, and seen that the city had been a centre of noble political and active economic life. In Alexander's time the city was no longer adequate as an organ for political and military administration, but it long continued to serve its purpose as a centre of economic life. The Greeks saw its rise, and they saw its relative decline. The fact that this change took place among Greek-speaking peoples and under Greek influence is one reason of the unique importance which Greece has in the economic history of the globe ; with the Greeks, city life attained its best development and also sank to its due subordination,—as an economic factor and not as a political unit. The experiments of organising government over large areas which were made by the Greeks were only partially successful ; they had but little stability, and they eventually succumbed before the advancing power of Rome ; but as experiments they are of supreme interest, since they gave the suggestion on which the Romans acted with greater success.

The history of Greek economic development gives us in a nutshell, as it were, the history of the world : there is seen the transition from natural to money economy, and the growth or modification of the three chief types of social organisation under monetary conditions. The same sort of transition has occurred in one country after another, and is continually taking place as new regions are being drawn into the circle of regular commercial intercourse. But no entirely new type of social organisation has been created ; the household, the city, and to a certain extent the empire—each with its own economic side—lay within the experience of the Greeks ; and to-day we have not outlived them.

The Romans on one hand, and the Christian Church on

the other, the era of discovery and the age of invention, have
served to modify the old institutions, but not to subvert them.
The main questions of household economy, of city economy
and of national economy which recur again and again, all came
within the cognisance of the Greeks.

There has of course been a great advance in all directions,
a great accumulation of experience, and a development of
more definite terminology[1] in which these problems may be
discussed ; but the economic literature of the Greeks in each
department was hardly superseded till a little more than a
century ago[2], when Adam Smith set the example of studying
economic phenomena without direct reference to political aims[3].
Xenophon's contributions to economic literature set the form
which others followed ; it is useful to compare his husbandry
with Varro, with Grosseteste or Fitzherbert ; while his discussion
of the revenue of Athens deals with much the same questions
as those which occupied French and English economic writers
in the seventeenth century, and deals with them in somewhat
the same way.

The book on *Economics*, which was mistakenly attributed to
Aristotle, is very fragmentary, but none the less interesting. It
recognises four kinds of Economy—regal, satrapical, political
and domestic. The treatment of household management presents no special features of interest. Regal Economy concerns
what we might call the prerogatives of the Crown—the coining
of money, the regulation of exports and imports, and the

---

[1] The doctrine of the 'balance of trade,' and the principles of the
'Mercantile System' do not appear to have been clearly formulated in
ancient times. Apparently it was under the experience of national rivalries
in the commerce of the modern world that they came into clear light. On
the neglect of these principles in the Roman Empire, see below, p. 187 n. 1.

[2] Compare the discussion in Aeschines, *Dial.* II. on the meaning of
riches and the character of the precious metals.

[3] On the special characteristic of Adam Smith and the precise nature of
his advance on his predecessors see my *Growth of English Industry*, II. 432.

supervision of administration. The satrapical economy is viewed as the administration of a province, and deals especially with the various kinds of taxation and the revenue which can be drawn from them. " Political " Economy is the management of municipal finance, and development of the resources of a city state. This subject is so fully dealt with by Aristotle himself in the *Politics, VII*[1], that we need the less regret that it is so slightly passed over by the later writers. There is no little interest, however, in the collection of expedients to obtain money adopted by different tyrants and potentates; they are recounted in the second book of *Economics*. Some of them were ingenious, some of them were merely dishonest, and some were both; the expedient of coining in brass or tin[2] and forcing it to pass as silver, was one to which rulers occasionally had recourse. Money economy had completely established itself, and the civil authorities succumbed before the temptation to tamper with the currency.

That many of the countries which subsequently rose into prominence worked out their economic destinies in practical independence is possible enough; but it is also true that Antioch, Alexandria, Marseilles and other centres of Greek civilization have never been wholly swept away, and that the Greek tradition has survived from age to age. Nor can we easily lay down the limits within which its actual influence was exerted. Here and there the links of connection between modern and classical civilization are clear enough; but the indirect dependence, which can only be obscurely traced, is not to be ignored. Just as all roads served to lead to Rome in the days of its Empire, so we find, in investigating the origins of our varied life in modern Christendom, that all lines of enquiry take us back to Greece.

[1] Book IV. according to Bekker's arrangement.
[2] *Economics*, II. 21, 24.

BOOK III.

ROME.

CHAPTER I.

THE STRUGGLE FOR SUPREMACY IN THE WEST.

46. In the Roman Empire the ambition which Alexander the Great had cherished was more than realised; that realm included a large part of the territory which he had acquired in the East, while it extended to lands in the West where his power had never been felt. Within the limits of the Empire, cities had been founded and were embraced, which continued to serve as centres of Hellenic culture; the effective security, which Roman rule established, gave an opportunity for the diffusion and perpetuation of Greek civilization. It is important to notice that the Roman empire was not created by the career of one brilliant general; it was slowly built up. This not improbably rendered it more stable; at any rate, attention may be directed to the material conditions which favoured the growth of a firmly consolidated empire.

The natural advantages of Carthage.

Military ambition was only gradually awakened in Rome, and it was chiefly called forth by the felt necessity for opposing the Carthaginians. The Romans came to be heirs of an immemorial feud; they succeeded to the Greek antagonism to the Phoenician, of which Pyrrhus had been the last exponent.

It had been the ambition of Pyrrhus to do in the West what Alexander had accomplished in the East; indeed, if he was less brilliant as a conqueror, he was perhaps more clearly inspired by other feelings besides the lust of conquest[1]. Carthage was the greatest representative of Semitic antagonism to Greece in the West, and the main object of Pyrrhus was to champion the Greek cause, to make it prevail throughout the whole of Sicily, and to humble the wealthy colony of Tyre. The failure of Pyrrhus was due to military and political reasons on which it is unnecessary to dwell; for the time it seemed as if Carthage must become supreme throughout the West, and as if the area into which Greek influence could not penetrate must be extended.

Carthage was the one barbarian city which by its long-continued freedom from internal revolution and its great wealth had won the admiration of Aristotle; it had many elements of strength, and these were skilfully utilised. Like all Phoenician colonies it had an admirable situation; there were two good natural harbours, and the town was strongly fortified[2]. A caravan route led through the north of Africa to the Temple of Jupiter Ammon, and thence to Ethiopia and the East; while there was also access by similar means across the desert to the gold and ivory producing districts of Africa. Carthage was excellently situated for trade both by land and sea : while the fertile plain in which she stood was admirably adapted for tillage. This seems to have been the art to which the Carthaginians devoted most attention; they had an ample food

---

[1] Pyrrhus was for some time a hostage at Alexandria in the reign of Ptolemy I and was connected by marriage with the Lagidae—two facts which emphasize his position in the history of Western development.

[2] Heeren, *Historical Researches* (African Nations), I. 29. Benson, *Cyprian*, xxvi f.

supply, and were able to export considerable quantities of corn to neighbouring cities.

Carthage was the one Phoenician colony which seems to have cherished political ambitions; she entered on a course of conquest in Africa and obtained a large tribute in kind, as well as levies in war from the Libyan and other tribes. Her political power gave her a superiority over older Phoenician settlements like Utica [1], and in regard to the numerous trading cities in which her citizens were settled on the African coast, she carefully restrained them from becoming in any sense her rivals. "By an extensive and ever-growing system of monopoly" they were excluded from the richest branch of trade— that with Spain ; they were not allowed to fortify themselves ; and their territory was so restricted that they seem to have been to some extent dependent for their food supply on corn exported from Carthage [2]. This jealous treatment of the colonies has some analogy in the policy which was adopted by Great Britain towards her dependencies in the eighteenth century. The naval and military force, which protected them against French interference, was provided by Great Britain, and it seemed fair to demand that they should not enter into hostile trading competition with the mother country ; an attempt was made to secure their allegiance by rendering them dependent upon her, not for food, but for manufactured goods.

The evidence in regard to Carthage, as in regard to Tyre, is very fragmentary, and is for the most part derived from foreign and hostile sources ; but there is reason to believe that the Carthaginians, like the Phoenicians, endeavoured to pursue an exclusive commerce, and to keep all rivals out of the field. This was partly desirable for the security of their fleets ; and their earliest commercial treaties, which survive, indicate an attempt to mark off the Roman sphere of influence from that of the Carthaginians. According to one of these treaties,

---

[1] Heeren, *Hist. Researches* (Africa), I. 42, 43.
[2] Heeren, *op. cit.* I. 39.

Romans were excluded from free trading with Sardinia and Libya; if, however, driven on these coasts by stress of weather, they were allowed to refit, but they were to sail again in five days[1]. The Carthaginians were still more jealous of the Massiliots[2]. In so far as the Carthaginians traded with Gaul, they had to use land routes, for the Greek settlements extended along the coast of Spain, and stretched towards the region where the valuable silver mines lay; the commerce of this region was guarded with special care. There were two lines of trade beyond the Straits of Gibraltar in which the Carthaginians appear to have had no seafaring rivals to contend with. They inherited the Phoenician trade from Gades to the Cassiterides—the Scilly Isles[3] or Cornwall—where they procured tin from the inhabitants. Another line of trade was opened up by a voyage of exploration along the West coast of Africa; the island of Cerne was an important mart and a centre for fishing, and trading relations of a primitive character were instituted with the desert tribes[4].

[1] Polybius, III. 22; Mommsen, I. 426, 442: II. 15. The treaty of 348 B.C. opened, that of 306 closed, the ports of Spain, Sardinia, and Libya to Roman vessels.

[2] Heeren, *op. cit.* I. p. 167.

[3] See the discussion in Heeren, *op. cit.* I. 168. The people of Massilia opened up, or perhaps reopened, an overland trade by the Rhone and imported British tin by this route. Diod. V. 38 (360).

[4] Herod. IV. 196. "The Carthaginians say also this, namely, that there is a place in Libya and men dwelling there, outside the Pillars of Heracles, to whom when they have come and have taken the merchandise forth from their ships, they set it in order along the beach and embark again in their ships, and after that they raise a smoke; and the natives of the country seeing the smoke come to the sea, and then they lay down the gold as an equivalent for the merchandise and retire to a distance away from the merchandise. The Carthaginians upon that disembark and examine it, and if the gold is in their opinion sufficient for the value of the merchandise, they take it up and go their way; but if not, they embark again in their ships and sit there; and the others approach and straight away add more gold to the former until they satisfy them: and they say that neither party wrongs the other; for neither do the Carthaginians lay

The value of this trade and of the natural advantages of the position of Carthage are most easily seen in the interval between the second and third Punic wars; even when her political power was broken she advanced so rapidly in wealth that the Romans feared she would rally her forces, and decided on extirpating the dreaded rival[1].

Carthage, like Athens, had such wealth as to give her not only independence but power; it does not appear, however, that the habit of money bargaining was so far in vogue within the community that there was opportunity for free political institutions. Economic freedom had not brought about the social conditions which render it possible for the poorer classes to participate in the rights and responsibilities of free citizenship. That they were familiar with the use of money is certain; it is even said that they had adopted a financial expedient of a very advanced type, and employed a token currency made of leather[2]. Whether the leather money of the Carthaginians was an ordinary institution, or a mere temporary expedient, does not appear; but it is most probable that they had recourse to it under some special circumstances. The best known instances of the use of leather money in more recent times— by Venice[3], and by Frederic II at the siege of Faenza[4]—were

hands on the gold until it is made equal to the value of their merchandise, nor do the others lay hands on the merchandise until the Carthaginians have taken the gold." (Macaulay.) Compare the Egyptian trading mentioned above, p. 26.

[1] The contributions of its subjects and the customs revenues completely covered the expenditure, so that no direct taxes were levied upon the citizens at any time, even when a yearly instalment of nearly £50,000 had to be paid to the Roman government; "fourteen years after the peace (of 202 B.C.) the state proffered immediate payment of the thirty-six remaining instalments." Mommsen, II. p. 20.

[2] Aeschines, *Dialog.* II. 24; Aristides, *Orat.* (Jebb) II. 145.

[3] In 1123, at Jaffa. Sanuto, *Vite de' Duchi di Venezia* in Muratori, XXII. 487.

[4] Villani, *Istorie Florentine*, V. 21.

merely temporary. At the same time it may be noticed that
the economic conditions in which Carthage flourished, as a self-
sufficing community with wealth constantly pouring in from
abroad, were exactly those in which a token money, or even
an inconvertible leather currency, could be easily introduced
and retained for internal circulation. Whether this occurred
or not, however, there was not such economic freedom—for
which money economy is an essential, though not the sole
condition—as to afford the inhabitants generally the requisite
leisure for political affairs.

47. Nor did the constitution of Carthage open up to those
who were citizens such opportunities of free
political activity as were available to citizens in
Greek cities. Ultimate decisions were indeed
referred to the people; but the ordinary affairs of state were
managed by a council in which the wealthy families had a
dominant part. Similarly, the whole of the judicial business
was decided by magistrates and not in popular tribunals; and
the mass of the citizens seem to have been practically excluded
from regular duties and responsibilities in political life. In
such a state of affairs there may have been stability and good
government; but there were not the opportunities for engaging
in active life, which rendered the mere possession of Athenian
citizenship a sort of liberal education. The Carthaginian
system had its advantages, but Athens produced better citizens
and masters of statecraft.

Their political and military system.

Nor was the citizen called on to discharge important duties
in war; the furnishing of the fleets was effected at the expense
of the public treasury; the galleys were manned by slaves, and
the vast armies which were brought into the field were partly
subjects and partly mercenaries. The citizens appear to have
formed one legion of special distinction, and also to have
served in the cavalry; but military commands were absorbed
by the richer families, and citizenship, as such, involved no
military duties. The vast armaments were procured and kept

in the field by public treasure; the strength of Carthage lay not in the stalwartness of her citizens, but in the length of her purse. The cruel punishments which were inflicted by the Carthaginians on unsuccessful generals would hardly have been meted out by comrades who had themselves served in the field; it was the revenge taken by disappointed masters on highly-paid servants for the loss of property. The composition of the Carthaginian army goes far to explain some points in the struggle with Rome; serious losses could be replaced sooner or later, so long as the money lasted and there were mercenaries to be hired; and the destruction of an army did not wound the city deeply. The lack of citizen veterans, who had served in the army, helps to account for the defenceless state of Carthage when attacked by Agathocles, and by Regulus. On the other hand, the rapid conquest of Spain, after the first Punic War, showed how great were the resources on which Carthage could rely. The Romans were justified in thinking that they could have no lasting security when the Carthaginians were once more accumulating the sinews of war, before the third and final struggle broke out. In spite of the material advantages and economic prosperity of Carthage, the Romans were able, by their military organisation and their statecraft, to destroy their rivals.

48. The main sources of revenue at Carthage were
Carthaginian similar to those which have been already dis-
plutocrats. cussed in regard to Athens,—from state-mines, from customs and trade, and from tribute; but there are some significant differences which may be pointed out. Private property appears to have played a far larger part at Carthage than at Athens, where the system of leasing public property was so common. The great families, like the Mago family, had very large estates in which large capitals were invested, and the fact is noticeable, even if we have not details enough to enable us to judge of its full significance. There was a narrower field for joint-stock speculation than at Athens;

but there was, on the other hand, a better opportunity for
building up great plutocratic families with hereditary possessions and powerful influence.   There was of course much land
in Attica in private hands; but the policy of the state was so
far unfavourable to the agricultural interest that landed proprietors did not accumulate increasing wealth.   In Carthage,
on the other hand, farming was a profitable field of enterprise;
and it is probable that permanent improvements were more
readily effected, that the management of land was better, and
the art of agriculture carried farther there, than among any
ancient people; the magnates had all the incentives which
arise from undisputed tenure and a good market for produce.
The Barca family are said to have been large proprietors of
mines; if this is so, they were in a position to control the
working of the mines more effectively than was done by the
Athenian democracy, who seem to have leased them out as
rapidly as they could.

The tribute of Carthage came partly from her own colonies
and partly from conquered peoples like the African tribes,
who brought large payments in kind.   This source of revenue
was greatly reduced after the second Punic War[1]; but the
receipts from customs continued to come in.   It would be of
interest if we knew more definitely what were the internal
arrangements for the conduct of trade, especially in those
commodities for which Carthage had a practical monopoly,
like Spanish silver, or British tin.   Was it left in private hands,
or was there any form of public organisation or authorised
association for carrying it on as a monopoly?   The practice of
other communities in carrying on distant trades would lead us
to expect that the Carthaginians had something analogous to
company trading; and the curious joint-trading with the
savages, described by Herodotus, renders it probable.

---

[1] Mommsen, II. p. 200.   Aided by the masterly inactivity of Rome,
Masinissa and the Numidian tribes were able to encroach further and
further upon Carthaginian territory.

However this may be, we can easily see that the resources of Carthage, as compared with those of Athens, were remarkably sound. There was less danger with regard to the food supply, since such ample arable lands lay at her very doors; while her policy was devised for the accumulation of wealth. "In fact, if government had resolved itself into a mere matter of business, never would any state have solved the problem more brilliantly than Carthage[1]." Even in the chief expenditure of the two states, there is a difference; Carthage seems to have done little for the sustenance and enjoyment of her citizens—unless the free tables are to be regarded as maintained by the state—but her wealth was not locked up in unremunerative public works; it was constantly employed. The main expenditure indeed was in war, and this is generally and rightly held to exhaust the material resources of a country; but Carthage carried on war as a trade, and on the whole made it pay. The conquest of new lands gave her an area from which she could draw tribute and could also obtain soldiers for fresh campaigns; while the products of these countries furnished new objects of trade. Her troops were drawn from every land, and her armies showed the greatest variety of equipment and weapons. The Libyan and Numidian cavalry furnished squadrons of great excellence; the Balearic slingers and the Gaulish swordsmen were effective in attack, while the elephants did good service in the field and in the baggage train. The army in the field was a signal demonstration of the wonders that can be wrought by the power of money.

49. Powerful as money is, it is not omnipotent; the treasure of Darius and his hordes of tributaries could not resist Alexander, and Carthage could not maintain herself against the discipline and undaunted determination of the Romans. In military matters money may do much, but the struggle really lies between men; and the Roman citizen was made of stern

Carthaginian influence in Rome.

---

[1] Mommsen, II. p. 20.

stuff. Nor was it a little thing for the future of Europe
that the issue between these cities turned out as it did, and
that Rome attained supremacy in the West. The Carthaginian, with his plutocratic government and his mercenary
troops hired to extend his avaricious power, was the very
embodiment of the greed of gain—ruthless and careless of
human life. The Carthaginian could never have been the
instrument of spreading Greek civilization, for he hated and
avoided it, as if it were a contamination; the Roman was in a
sense a barbarian too, but he had the grace to admire the
culture he did not himself possess. The victory of Rome
broke down the barrier of aggressive barbarism, and indirectly
gave scope for the freer spread of Greek influence in the
world[1].

The Roman was far less conscious of any mission to
spread Greek civilization than Pyrrhus, or even than Alexander;
his love of conquest for its own sake was more unalloyed; but
the fact remains that the attempt to organise and maintain
Roman rule necessitated a diffusion of the arts of civilised life.
Roman conquest brought about a new expansion of Hellenism;
it was from Greece that the Romans derived much of their
inspiration in literature and art; it was from the Greeks they
appropriated much of their skill in administration and finance.
But the civilization which was diffused under Roman rule was
not purely Greek; those who eventually inherited the mastery
of the world were debtors not only to the Greek, but also to
the Phoenician; and this at second hand as well as directly.
Skill in the manual arts had been developed and diffused by
the Phoenicians, and it was partly from them that the Greeks
had acquired it; but there were many arts which the Romans
derived direct from the Phoenicians of Carthage and not from
Hellenic pupils of Tyrian teachers[2].

---

[1] For a comparison of Carthage and Rome as ruling cities see Freeman,
Historical Essays, vol. IV. pp. 6, 7.

[2] There were of course various arts which were not borrowed from

The arts of shipbuilding and of naval warfare were entirely unknown to the Romans until they were forced to take them up in the struggle for Sicily with which the Punic Wars began. In this particular department the steps of the progress are interesting: the Greeks with their triremes improved on the Phoenician biremes; the Carthaginians improved on the Greek model with their quinqueremes, and this type was in turn copied by the Romans. The rapidity with which they turned the tables on their masters, and the success of their newly-invented grappling-irons, show how readily they came to understand and to assimilate the conditions of warfare on the new element.

The second art which in its improved and scientific form came to the Romans from the Carthaginians was that of husbandry. The Greek and, at first, the Roman, managed his estate like a gentleman with reference to the requirements of his household; the Carthaginian pursued agriculture as a profitable trade. This fashion was taken up in Rome, and the *latifundia* on the Campagna became more general during the Punic Wars; they were the Roman reproduction of the Carthaginian model, capitalist estates worked for a profit[1]. Among the very few fragments of Carthaginian literature which have survived are portions of Mago's treatise on husbandry. It was a work which was much admired, and from which Roman writers diligently copied. The knowledge of Punic tillage had reached Rome at the very time when the conditions of her rural districts rendered it possible to carry it into effect.

either; they may be ascribed to the Etruscans; such was their method of surveying and laying out cities (see above, p. 132, *n.* 5), and the tradition as to the early organisation of the dyers, suggests that this trade also was independent of Greek influence. Blümner, *Technologie,* I. 216.

[1] The oldest trace of centralised farming may be seen in the enactment of 367 B.C. which requires the employment of a certain proportion of free labourers with slaves. Appian (*Bell. Civ.* I. 7—10) certainly represents the *latifundia* as an evil of gradual growth: and it was allowed to grow until remedies were found to be more dangerous than the disease. Mommsen, I. p. 457; II. 362—393.

CHAPTER II.

THE ROMAN REPUBLIC.

50. THE gradual growth of the military power before which Carthage succumbed, and by which a military empire was effectively established in the ancient world, presents many features of economic interest. It will suffice however to lay stress on those points which serve to indicate how Roman development differed from that of Athens and Carthage, so that she was enabled to maintain the sovereignty at which they grasped for a time.

Common interests and mutual agreements.

One striking physical difference, which contributed to the stability of Roman rule before the struggle with Carthage, though in the end it proved a weakness to the Roman Empire[1], lay in the fact that her ambitions were fixed on the land, and not on dominion by sea. The Roman power was extended slowly and bit by bit through Latium, and over the Etruscans and Italians, till the whole of the peninsula was brought to acknowledge it. The Athenians and their allies had joined to co-operate on the sea, and the control of the sea gave the Athenians a superiority over the allies; the Carthaginians by the same means could keep their colonies in subjection and dependence. The sea power could be used by each of them from the first, but not by Rome until she had secured the

---

[1] See below, p. 190.

control of Italy by land. The city of the seven hills lay in an open plain, and it was the ambition of the Romans to extend the area which they controlled, so as to lessen the dangers of hostile attack. It may even be said that the motive of Rome in her first advances was the humble one of making defensive alliances so as to secure immunity from hostile invasion; she did not at first desire to conquer her neighbours or reduce them to submission. Athens with her wooden walls and scientific frontier had physical safeguards; Rome was driven to obtain by treaty and agreement a security which was not accorded her by her natural position.

Since this was the object of her policy in her dealings with her neighbours, it helped to a considerable extent to determine the character of those dealings. She aimed at attracting each city or community or tribe to herself, and at keeping them, however much they might be akin in race, from uniting with one another to oppose her. It was with this object that the Latin colonies were founded, as military fortresses which might prevent the junction of hostile neighbours; and the differences of privilege among those who were admitted to her friendship left them less likely to unite among themselves. It would have been absolutely suicidal for Rome to impose any badge of subjection, such as the payment of a tribute[1]. The constant pressure of a common burden would have been a continual incentive to the allies to combine, in order to throw off a yoke which pressed on all alike. By treating them, not as subjects but as allies, who were not branded with any mark of servitude and who had freedom to manage their own internal affairs, she built up a federation in which she maintained the political and military supremacy[2]. But it was more than a federation: each

---

[1] See above, p. 115. Mommsen, I. 804. The tax known as *tributum* at Rome was of a different character. The *tributum* was a tithe, raised when required, to pay the soldiers: it was levied on *res mancipi* and after successful wars was sometimes repaid.

[2] Beloch, *Ital. Bund*, 203.

of the allies participated to a larger or smaller extent in the privileges which Romans enjoyed, not so much in political power as in social status; while each, as time went on, had something to gain from the protection of a powerful neighbour against those who threatened them by land or by sea[1]. There were ties formed by commercial intercourse and family connection which bound many of them to the capital, but no similar links were permitted to connect the various allies with one another. Yet while each of the allied cities was thus bound to Rome, and under Roman rule in political and military affairs, each was allowed to maintain its own customs and, so far as possible, its own constitution. This communal autonomy was a much more real freedom in Italy than it had been in Greece, since there was no exaction of tribute; the magistrates of the towns in all probability preserved a considerable measure of judicial authority, though the Prefects administered justice in the districts where no local magistracy existed, and cases of many kinds must have been transferred on appeal to Rome.

The ties which connected Rome with the neighbouring Latin cities were shaken by the success of the Gauls; but their strength was clearly shown in the Samnite wars, when the power of numerous and vigorous tribes was broken, chiefly, as it seems, by the cohesion of the Roman system and the inability of her Samnite, Etruscan and Celtic foes to co-operate steadily against her. Her success in the third Samnite war enabled her to extend her power to the very south of Italy, and to draw under her shield the flourishing cities which had long before been planted as Greek colonies in Magna Graecia. From the beginning of the third century B.C. the Romans had within their control, and were in constant official communication with, a string of cities stretching from Naples round the coast, and were thus brought into more direct contact with the arts of life as cultivated in Greece. That they had earlier trading connections is certain, for we find in their monetary

[1] Mommsen, I. 360.

and other terms[1], and their metric system, indubitable evidence
of the influence of Greek merchants.   These towns, however,
furnish the earliest instances of Greek communities continuing
to live and flourish under the shield of Roman protection, and
form the most obvious links of connection between Roman
and Greek civilization at this early time.

It was not till Rome had established her dominion by land
that she appeared as a competitor for maritime empire, and
aspired to conquer lands beyond the sea.   It is worth while to
note the special characteristics of her power in Italy.   It did
not rest on her natural advantages, nor on her acquired wealth,
but on common interests and mutual agreements.   Her power
was built on a moral, not merely on a material basis; it was
not that she had sufficient resources to enable her to keep
other peoples in subjection, but she had welded them together,
under her own leadership as predominant partner, into a body
politic, throughout which there was considerable immunity
from outside attack, and internal maintenance of law and
order, while there was still the fullest possible scope for the
free policy of each of the several parts.   These are exactly the
conditions which afford the best opportunity for economic
progress; and this model was steadily kept in view as Roman
conquest spread and Roman government extended beyond the
limits of Italy.

51.   The constant warfare in which Rome was engaged in
the conquest of Italy was a serious tax on her
resources.   War can be used, as the Carthaginians used it, as the means of obtaining plunder
and tribute; but this, from the conditions of their territory,
and the nature of their policy, the Romans were unable to do.
For them war was a continual strain, which brought no direct
profit, except in so far as they were able to obtain additional
domain and to plant some military colonies.   Even this was a

The effects
of the wars in
Italy.

---

[1] Mommsen, I. 206.

drain upon the element of national strength on which war told most severely—the population.

It has been pointed out above that the armies of Carthage were largely composed of mercenaries, and that the destruction of one of these armies meant the loss of her money, but not of her men. The armies of the Roman republic were on the other hand composed of citizen soldiers, and the burden of military duty was incompatible with the effective farming of their own land. The pressure of military service told seriously; but the causes which had brought about the decay of the free rural proprietors in Attica were also potent in Rome. From a very early time the policy of the city favoured a cheap food supply, and this resulted necessarily in the depression of the agricultural interest, and especially of the small farmer. After the period of the second Macedonian war the Roman soldiers were habitually maintained by food imported from abroad, and supplies of corn from Spain and Sicily were sold to the populace at unremunerative prices[1]. In the earlier era the citizen-farmer had to fear the competition of the wealthy men who had taken up large areas of the public domain and cultivated it with slave labour. The Licinian laws were intended to strike a double blow at this class, by limiting the number of *jugera* which any man might hold, and by insisting that capitalist farmers should hire half the labour required, so as to provide a field for the employment of citizens. The other enactment, which treated payments of interest as instalments of the capital borrowed[2], would favour the small farmer even more effectually than Solon's legislation had done. But the whole of the economic tendencies of the time were against them. They could not attempt to carry on the more profitable branches of tillage in vineyards and olive[3] gardens, which supplied products

---

[1] Mommsen, II. 371.

[2] Mommsen, I. 304.

[3] Mommsen, II. 370, 375.

for export[1]; pasture farming also required capital, and was the resource of wealthy men; and the increasing importation of corn deprived them of a market for produce. The recurring difficulties, which the agrarian laws of the Gracchi[2] and of Caesar were designed to check, only serve to show how deep-seated were the causes of the agricultural depression which subverted the free peasantry and drove them to the towns, while the lands were utilised as large runs or farms by wealthy speculators. The results of the whole movement were shown in the disastrous decline of the free population, from whom soldiers could be drawn for the legions. The disappearance of the free peasantry opened the way for the organisation of husbandry in large estates on the Carthaginian model.

In the rise of the *equites*, who came to engross so much judicial authority, and who provided a body of cavalry for the Roman armies[3], we have at least an interesting analogy with the Carthaginian plutocracy. Men of the same type rise to similar positions both magisterial and military. Whether there was any conscious imitation of the Punic model in this case (as there probably was in regard to tillage), or not, it is at least interesting to notice that as Rome entered on her career of conquest outside Italy she came to approximate more, both in the management of the soil, and in some constitutional matters, to the Carthaginian type.

52.   The material products, like the olive, which we

---

[1] Mommsen, I. 211. The landed aristocracy owned ships to export wine, and possibly imported rather than produced corn.

[2] Ihne, *Rome*, IV. 385. In the case of Ti. Gracchus the difficulties were (1) what was to become of the slave-class if their employment was taken? (2) what was the benefit to poor citizens if the slaves were emancipated? (3) what was to be the scheme of compensation to present occupiers?

[3] Ihne, *Rome*, IV. 104. The paid cavalry must be distinguished from the old knights of the eighteen centuries: but the paid class became more and more privileged, and had less actual service to perform. Up till the time of C. Gracchus however, there was no equestrian census.

associate most closely with Italy, appear to have been introduced under Greek influence, and the methods of ad- Government ministration which had been organised in Attica by contractors. found a congenial soil in Italy and developed in complexity, and in the magnitude of the transactions[1]. All public works and undertakings of every kind were let to contractors ; the full results of this policy only appeared when it was applied to the government of the provinces[2], but it was completely developed as a method of administration before the Roman dominion extended outside Italy.

There was no tribute to be farmed like that which accrued to Athens, but the duty of collecting the rents from the public domain was regularly put up to auction. In similar fashion, the army and navy contractors fitted out ships and made provision for armies in the field, while the public works like the Via Appia and the aqueducts which brought water to Rome were carried out by contractors who employed slave labour. The tenure of the magisterial offices was so short, that there was no other way in which works of this kind could be more satisfactorily organised and carried out than by letting them to private capitalists.

While so much scope was given for the operations of moneyed men in ordinary business, there was also a large class of capitalists who were willing to undertake public service. Though the Italian wars of Rome were not remunerative to the state, they furnished booty that was remunerative to indi-viduals, and any citizen who started with a little hoard was able to find means to employ it. The usurer would make advances to the small farmer or the craftsman ; or the owner of a small capital could combine with others to make loans on bottomry. The system of association was well understood,

---

[1] Mahaffy, *Social Life in Greece*, 408.

[2] On the distinction between *publicani* and *negotiatores*, see Deloume, *Les manieurs d'argent à Rome*, p. 93. The whole book is an admirable study of the financial system at Rome during this period.

and every Roman was an adept at book-keeping and made careful entries of all his transactions.

There was a high standard of business accuracy; but the avarice which characterised Carthaginian policy asserted itself unchecked in the private affairs of the Romans. The extortions of usurers were the subject of frequent execration, and certain forms of business were prohibited; but it was not easy to enforce these prohibitions, and the greed of gain was a dominant influence in transactions of every kind. The extent to which wrong might be done in private circles is most easily gathered from the stories which show the lack of public spirit. That the contractors, who were supplying the Roman troops in Sicily with food, should sink their ships in order to obtain the sum assured to them by the state was bad enough, but that it should be so difficult to obtain a conviction against them, though their crime was notorious, is still more discreditable to the Roman Senate[1]. In all this we can see the seeds of that general corruption which disgraced the Roman republic in its dealings with subject peoples. The principles of government might be sound, the treatment of allies conciliatory, and the forms of law favourable to industrial progress; but the affairs of state were a field where unbridled private rapacity had free play.

53. When the Roman republic started on its career of conquest beyond the limits of Italy, the principles of policy remained the same, though they had to be applied in a new fashion, and the existing defects in the administrative methods became more glaring when they were exhibited on a large scale. The power of Rome was consolidated by treaties, on more or less favourable terms, with certain communities, and by organising the government of intervening areas.

The Provinces.

The principal communities which had rights and privileges accorded by treaty were the flourishing cities[2] that had been

---

[1] Livy, xxv. 2, 3.   [2] Mitteis, *Reichsrecht.*, 86.

planted as Greek colonies, or in some cases that had been established by Phoenicians. At various points on or near the shores of the Mediterranean there were cities which secured a formal independence and a real self-government. Such were Cadiz, Marseilles, Messina and Athens (*civitates foederatae*); while others were free from fiscal burdens (*immunes*), like Utica, Smyrna and Ephesus; a still larger number were preserved in the Roman provinces on less favourable terms[1].

As the Roman rule extended there were increased opportunities for peaceful communication and commercial development, but the internal life and institutions of these towns, as industrial centres, were but little affected; Marseilles[2] continued to be a centre of Greek life and thought, and served as a channel by which a Hellenising influence was brought to bear on Gaul[3], as it was gradually subdued. That the alliances of these cities with Rome sometimes paved the way for subsequent absorption is true enough, as in the case of Rhodes. The friendship of Rome was a costly privilege, and those who resented its exacting character, were too likely to be forced into complete subjection. But in one form or another the process went on; and by including these maritime cities within her dominion Rome attained to a maritime supremacy such as

---

[1] Ihne, IV. 198.

[2] At the time of the Christian era Marseilles was a recognised centre of Greek culture to which Romans resorted for the sake of education. Strabo, IV. 5 (181). The writings of Irenaeus, and the special heresies he had to meet, show how completely it retained this character at the close of the second century. On its history as a Greek town under the Roman Empire compare Hirschfeld, *Gall. Stud.* in *Sitzungsberichte der Wiener. Acad.* (1885), CIII. p. 281 f. Marseilles was still spoken of as a Greek city when it succumbed to the barbarians (νῦν ἐξ Ἑλληνίδος ἐστὶ βαρβαρικὴ, Agathias, *Hist.* I. 2); the district was long known as *Graecia*, and the Gulf of Lyons as a *mare Graecum*. Kiepert, *Alte Geog.* 506, *n.* 4.

[3] Ut non Graecia in Galliam emigrasse, sed Gallia in Graeciam translata videretur. Justin, *Hist.* XLIII. 4. The types of and inscriptions on coins show that the Gauls derived this art from Greek sources and probably from the Massiliots. Sonny, *De Massiliensium rebus quaestiones*, 107.

no other people had enjoyed. The southern Mediterranean had been the Phoenician, the northern had been the Grecian water; but both came under the influence of Rome.

It has been pointed out that the gradual extension of the Roman federation in Italy may be regarded as an attempt to secure immunity from attack, when no physical barrier afforded protection. It seems at first sight as if there could be no similar excuse for the policy, on which the Republic entered with such hesitation, of acquiring sovereignty by sea, or in the lands beyond the sea; we are ready to ascribe it to a lust of conquest like that which actuated Alexander, though it is not easy to see how the desire to win reputation which actuates a soldier personally should affect the policy of a people. It should be remembered, however, that there is a sense in which the transmarine wars of Rome may be said to have been undertaken at least partly in self-defence. Rome was becoming dependent on foreign countries for her food supply; to have Sicily and Sardinia under her own control, rather than that of her possible enemies, was coming to be a matter of vital importance; the rich lands, in which Carthage stood, offered a very special temptation to hungry citizens. The first step of interference in Sicily appears to have been taken, far less from any scheme of ambition, than in the hope of disarming the possible hostility of Mamertine raiders and pirates. However this may be, it is interesting to notice that when Rome extended her ambition from supremacy in Italy to sovereignty in the Mediterranean, she took over a coast that was already sprinkled with centres of Greek civilization. An examination of names and terms serves to show how deeply the social system of Rome, even within Italy, was impregnated by Greek influence; and it needs no proof to see that, so far as her power on the sea was concerned, she did but incorporate into her system what the Greeks had already established.

This period of transmarine expansion also differs from the extension of Roman power in Italy, inasmuch as large areas were organised as conquered territory. The lands taken in Italian wars had been added to the public domain and leased to the citizens; but in the provinces the more common practice was to allow the old inhabitants to remain on condition of paying a tribute[1]. This was the oriental method of dealing with conquered territory, and the Romans only carried on the existing practice in exacting a tribute from lands that had formerly belonged to Carthage or to Macedon. Indeed the tribute exacted by the Roman people was by no means heavy as compared with the demands of the rulers they superseded; but it was a permanent badge of servitude to which the Italian peoples had not been forced to submit.

The expansion of Rome in the Mediterranean lands was really governed by the same principles which had led to its extension in Italy. Doubtless there were proconsuls who were ambitious of military reputation, but there is comparatively little evidence of wanton aggression by the Roman state; it was, in fact, an extension rendered necessary for self-defence in changed conditions. In precisely the same way, the preservation of other alien communities in their rights and privileges was apparently a generous policy, and the hardships inflicted in republican times were not due to public oppression but to public neglect. The State provided no adequate securities against official rapacity and the private greed of Roman capitalists.

54. The class of moneyed men, who contracted for the business of state, enjoyed a certain amount of protection from outside competition. The senatorial aristocracy were restricted to shipping the produce of their estates, and were prevented from taking part in speculation; and the allies do not appear to have had a footing in the Roman money-market. At the same time, it is unlikely that such restrictions could be enforced, or that those who wished for them failed to get shares in the great capitalist associations which exploited the provinces.

The Publicani and Negotiatores.

[1] Cf. note on p. 152.

The *publicani* were the most prominent of capitalists, since they dealt with the State; they found the money for carrying on the business of every department of State. The public works of the royal period had been executed under political compulsion, but the state-contractors came to the front in the earlier times of the Republic, and dominated everywhere in the third and second centuries B.C.[1]

The tribute of the provinces, whether it was rendered in money or in corn, was a favourable field for their operations. In the collection there was an opportunity for the extortionate gains which made the 'publican' a by-word among the Jews; and in the transmission of money or produce to Rome there was also a chance of profitable speculation. The mines of Spain, and of all the countries which the Greeks and Phoenicians had visited, also came gradually to form part of the estate of the Roman Republic; and these, as well as the quarries of every sort, were worked by the *publicani* as contractors. There were others who collected the revenue from public pastures, or farmed the customs. It was the policy of the Romans to secure the command of the provinces by laying out their great military roads; even in cases where no other public works were undertaken, this was a necessary labour. In this department, as well as in the construction of harbours or basilicas, the same method was employed.

The capital was provided by associations, which had their centre in Rome; the proprietors and the shareholders cared chiefly for their dividends, and felt no sense of responsibility as to the manner in which these dividends were obtained. The worst abuses may have existed in the mines and public works, as there was no restriction, either in public opinion or law, on the overworking of the slaves and criminals; and even if there had been, it would have been difficult to enforce. In regard to the illegal extortions in collecting the tribute, little redress was possible; the magistrates on the spot

[1] Polybius, VI. 17.

had friendly relations with the *publicani*, which they were unlikely to disturb[1]; while the cases of appeals to Rome came
before the *equites*, that is to say, the very class by whom and
in whose interest these depredations were practised.

The evil results of this system were seen most appallingly
in the devastation of the provinces, especially of Sicily, which
had been subjected to it for the longest period; the greater
part of the island, with the exception of Syracuse and
Messina, was governed by a Roman praetor from the close
of the second Punic war. The tithe of agricultural produce
was not a heavier burden than that which the country had
borne before it came into Roman hands[2]; but the rapacity
of the collectors seems to have pressed so heavily, that large
areas went out of cultivation, and the towns fell into pre-
mature decay. The detail of the methods by which this ruin
was wrought has been exhibited by a master-hand in Cicero's
Verrine Orations.

There were, however, many fields for the private enterprise
of *negotiatores*, besides the operations that were undertaken
as Government contracts by the *publicani*. Transactions with
half-civilized or uncivilized peoples have always supplied a
favourite field for the operations of the moneyed man; and
on the fringe of the Roman provinces, and among the allies,
there were tribes and peoples who had commerce with Rome,
though they were not formally subject to her. Of their
dealings we know little or nothing, though the analogy of
the treatment of Indian races by white men is at least sug-
gestive. There is, perhaps, a sufficient suggestion in the fact
that the frontier troubles of Rome so often began with quarrels
in which the *negotiatores* were concerned. They were deeply
engaged in transactions in Gaul[3], and goaded the people to
the insurrection which began with the massacre of *negotiatores*

---

[1] Cicero, *ad Familiares*, XIII. ix. 2.

[2] Ihne, IV. 208.

[3] Cicero, *pro Fonteio*, I.

at Genabum; a similar cause was at work in bringing about
the war with Mithridates[1]. Even in a comparatively poor
province, like Sardinia, the Roman *foeneratores* found the opportunity of plying their trade—probably in lending money to
distressed agriculturists on the security of their lands.

In the first century B.C., Rome was the monetary centre
of the world, inasmuch as the capital, which was engaged in
public administration or private business all over the known
world, was owned in Rome. The associations of capitalists
were carefully organized; some of them were partnerships of
wealthy men, and some were joint-stock companies which were
managed on behalf of the shareholders by *participes*[2]. A very
large portion of the Roman population had shares in these
undertakings; and the Forum, with its *basilicae*, may be regarded as an immense stock-exchange where monetary speculation of every kind was continually going on. There are
those who complain of the evil effects of stock-exchange
speculation, of the irresponsibility of directors and shareholders in the present day, of the pressure brought to bear
on Egypt by the bond-holders, and so forth. But these
phenomena, regrettable as they are, may help us in some
measure to realise the state of things in the Roman Republic,
when the policy of the government was controlled by the
stock-exchange, when the provinces were ruled in the interests of the stock-exchange, and judicial appeals were decided
by the stock-exchange. There was a subordination of public
duty to private interests throughout the whole world, such as
has been equalled perhaps, but never surpassed, even in the
worst times of the Tammany domination in New York.

55. Had the Manchester school had an elementary acquaintance with Roman history, they could
hardly have assumed as axiomatic the prin-
ciple that the freedom for capitalists to pursue their individual
interest necessarily results in the well-being of the com-

Lack of
official control.

---

[1] Deloume, *op. cit.* 94.   [2] Deloume, *op. cit.* 155.

munity. Of the energy and enterprise of Roman *publicani* and *negotiatores* there can be no doubt; they opened up the resources of the ancient world and established communication between its various parts; but this enterprise was not an unalloyed good. It is only under very special conditions, including the existence of a strong government to exercise a constant control, that free play for the formation of associations of capitalists bent on securing profit, is anything but a public danger. The landed interest in England has hitherto been strong enough to bring legislative control to bear on the moneyed men from time to time; it is an interesting speculation how far such control can be sufficiently exercised in the newer lands—like the United States and Australia— where there is no similar tradition. The problem of leaving sufficient liberty for the formation of capital and for enterprise in the use of it[1], without allowing it license to exhaust the national resources has not been solved.

It was the disgrace of the Roman people in the time of the Republic that they made no attempt to solve this problem. The crowd in the Forum was too far away, and too little informed as to the condition of the provinces, to be likely to take it to heart, even if it had been inclined to do so. The attitude of the officials in the provinces is much more instructive. They must have been aware of the mischief that was at work, but many of them were entirely careless in the matter and made no effort to bring their authority to bear; while it appears that the exceptional men who had the will to take a sound course in checking the evil[2] were soon deprived of the power to act.

[1] On the danger of checking these altogether, see below, p. 186.

[2] Q. Mucius Scaevola (praetor of Asia in 98 B.C.) appears to have been doubly exceptional, as he was not only most popular in his province, but was also held up as a model to his successors by the Senate. Valerius Maximus, VIII. 15. 6. It was a proof of almost 'divine virtue' to be so successful. Cicero, *ad Quintum fratrem*, I. i. 33.

The Roman governor, with only a limited term of office, and with no salary to recoup him for his expenses in securing his position, was under the direct temptation to use his power in his own personal interests[1]. In those regions, which were imperfectly organised, the opportunity of misrule was greatest, and the direct responsibility lay, not with *publicani*, but with the governors. Spain[2] was one of the districts which gave the greatest opportunity for the amassing of private fortunes; while the Praetors of Sardinia could combine pleasure with profit by organizing slave-raids on the hills, and exporting their booty to the markets at Rome. Such men were not likely to keep the ulterior prosperity of the province in mind, or to interfere with the operations of capitalists when their conduct was endangering it.

The most striking story of all, however, reaches us from the province of Asia. Lucullus was responsible for the administration in B.C. 70, after an enormous war-indemnity had been imposed on the province by Sulla. The attempt to raise the arrears of tithe and the sum of 20,000 talents in addition, threw the whole country into the hands of the Roman *negotiatores*; Lucullus set himself not only to keep the province at peace and to guard against frontier foes, but to impose a check upon the demands of the usurers. The description of the manner in which their claims were enforced is instructive[3];

---

[1] Ihne, IV. 203.   [2] *Ibid.*, III. 378; IV. 206.

[3] Plutarch, *Lucullus*, cc. VII. and XX. "These (the *publicani*) Lucullus drove away like so many harpies, which robbed the poor inhabitants of their food." They had to sell "the most beautiful of their sons and daughters, the ornaments and offerings in their temples, their paintings and the statues of their gods. The last resource was to serve their creditors as slaves. Their sufferings prior to this were more cruel and insupportable, prisons, racks, tortures, &c., insomuch that servitude seemed a happy deliverance....The public fine which Sylla had laid upon Asia was twenty thousand talents. It had been paid twice; and yet the merciless collectors, by usury upon usury, now brought it to a hundred and twenty thousand talents. These men, pretending they had been unjustly treated, raised a clamour in Rome.......they had indeed a considerable interest, because

Lucullus put an end to illegal oppression, and reduced the demands for interest within the legal limits. These were the crimes which led the Roman people to refuse to reappoint an excellent soldier to command, and induced them to transfer the province to Pompeius, the nominee of the capitalist classes[1]. When such things were possible, the forms of treaty and law were absolutely worthless as giving any security for general progress. The classes who had sent Pompeius to the East had probably no reason to complain of his interference with their proceedings, and he also contrived to make his operations in Asia the means of his own advance to the summit of his fortunes.

56. There was indeed one sphere in which the interests of Roman capitalists told in favour of good government; it was necessary for their operations that there should be frequent intercourse with distant places, and many of them were engaged in maritime commerce. So soon as the greater part of the Mediterranean came under the control of one power, piracy and privateering were looked upon as forms of enterprise immediately injurious to the public, and as such they were put down. Pompeius had earned the gratitude of the inhabitants of Rome before they placed him in power in Asia, for he had in a few months broken up the gangs of pirates and thus facilitated commercial intercourse in the Mediterranean. The decree, under which Pompeius was commissioned, gave him extraordinary authority over the whole of the Mediterranean waters and along the coasts for a range of about fifty miles inland, but the occasion demanded extraordinary measures. The head-quarters of the pirates were on the coast of Cilicia, and they had something like a thousand galleys, splendidly fitted out. They not only waylaid fleets, but plundered the most sacred shrines and

The repression of piracy.

many persons who had a share in the administration were their debtors." (Langhorne.)

[1] Cicero, *pro lege Manilia*, VI. VII.

ravaged the coast of Italy. The urgent need for prompt action was made palpable by the manner in which the corn fleets were threatened; there was an imminent danger of famine, and the immediate effect of the passing of the decree was a fall in the price of corn at Rome. This confidence was amply justified; Pompeius, who was well supported by his lieutenants, divided the whole sea into thirteen parts, and set about clearing the waters between Rome and Africa, Sicily, Sardinia and Corsica. This was successfully accomplished in forty days, and "superabundant plenty reigned in the markets[1]" when Pompeius passed through Rome on his way to Brundisium, whence he sailed with sixty galleys to the coast of Cilicia. A battle ensued in which the pirates were defeated; they subsequently capitulated, and were deported to inland districts, where lands were assigned them and they were under no temptation to resume their depredations by sea. This task, which was accomplished in little more than three months, reflects the greatest credit on Pompeius, and deservedly raised him to a high position in the favour of the commercial classes and populace at Rome. He had the misfortune to live on past the zenith of his greatness, and his name is clouded by his ultimate failure; but in the splendour of his schemes both by land and sea, and the rapidity of his combinations, he showed himself but little inferior to Alexander the Great; whilst he also demonstrated how feasible it was for a man with military talents and striking personality to raise himself to supreme power under the forms of a republican government.

57.   The Roman Republic was indeed condemned, and it was inevitable that some other form of government should take its place. It had obviously failed in the two points which had lain at the foundation of all Roman prosperity.

Constant war and chronic in-security.

(i)   One condition which the Romans aimed at securing, was that of immunity from attack; they had made war in

[1] Plutarch, *Pompeius*, 27.

order to procure peace, and a guarantee for peace. But their dominion had become the prey of ambitious generals who led rival legions against one another. So long as a popular leader had the unfettered command of a distant province, there was at least the danger that he would build up a power which should make him an object of envy to other generals and a danger to the republic. The risk of attack from without seemed to be gone, but there was little hope of immunity from war at home.

(ii) The second point, on which the well-being of the Roman dominion had rested, was the maintenance of law and order; this may be gathered from the freedom that was given to the allied communities, and the enforcement of law by Roman Praetors in other areas. The story of the maladministration of the provinces shows how entirely this condition of economic prosperity was lacking. The *publicani* and *negotiatores* were exhausting the most fertile areas; the private ambition of the generals induced chronic warfare, and the private greed of the speculators rendered the cultivation of the soil or the maintenance of industry a hopeless task. The pressing need of society was the establishment of peace, and the maintenance of such order that agriculture and the arts of life might revive. Only by the successful assumption of universal dominion could the dangers from ambitious generals be abated; only by the establishment of a strong personal rule and a reformed administration could internal order be secured. Octavius showed his genius by the skill and diplomacy with which he waited for and used his opportunity; he was able to build up a system of personal government which was so strong, and so indubitably necessary, that it survived numberless attacks and maintained its dignity, despite the disgrace which attaches to many of his successors. In the Roman Empire the dream of Alexander was realised, and realised under conditions which gave it an extraordinary permanence, and enabled it to exercise the most marvellous influence on the destinies of the world.

CHAPTER III.

THE ROMAN EMPIRE.

58. DURING the forty-one years of his rule, Augustus
Fiscal administration. framed a system of administration which effectually limited abuses that had been universal under the Republic. By keeping the military authority and the administration of the most important provinces in his own hands, he prevented any successful general from cherishing the hope of ousting him or from securing resources which would enable him to make the attempt. By organising an effective public administration, and developing an official class, he rendered it less necessary for government to carry on public business through the agency of contractors. This was the positive advance which he made. So far as household management or municipal government was concerned, there was little left for the Romans to do; but the problem of administering an empire under monetary conditions, though it had been the subject of some experiments, was still unsolved. Augustus set himself to face it with such success that the scheme which his genius devised, as perfected by his successors, not only afforded a weary world an unexampled period of rest and prosperity, but formed a model which has been consciously or unconsciously reproduced in mediaeval and modern states. He drew up a budget and shaped a financial system which gave remarkable stability to the Empire, even under unworthy rulers; he organised the affairs of state in a monetary form, and endeavoured to guard against what was arbitrary or unfair.

He was not content to utilise the machinery which was already in operation for Roman finance. The *aerarium Saturni* into which the receipts from the Senatorial provinces were paid, was maintained. It remained nominally under senatorial authority, though the Emperors soon came to exercise a practical control both in the appointment of officials and the disposition of revenue. Various branches of income were gradually transferred to the *fiscus* which was the main financial organ of the Empire; it had been created by Augustus, and was under the personal direction of the Emperor[1]. The type of economic institution, on which the new administrative machinery was modelled, was not that of a city, but of a household[2].

It was the staff of the Caesar's household that managed the Empire, and founded the various departments of state. The Romans, as has been said above, kept their private accounts with scrupulous accuracy; and Augustus applied the same sort of care to the enormous domain which had come under his charge[3]. The development of a sovereign's household into an administrative system is a process that has recurred again and again—e.g. under Charles the Great, and in England. It was a particularly fortunate expedient at Rome in the time of Augustus.

The remains, which are in some ways most characteristic of the Empire, bear fitting witness to this fact. In imperial Rome we have a series of great palaces; the Forum tells of the busy life of the speculators of the Republic, but the Palatine displays the house of the Emperor of the world. Still, it is not in Rome that the best work of the greatest period of the Empire is to be seen; that lies far scattered in every land where Roman armies had gone, and where the reformed administration enabled the Flavian and succeeding emperors to develop the resources of their vast estate. The rampart which runs from Newcastle to Carlisle is a monument of their

[1] Marquardt, *Römische Staatsverwaltung*, II. 295.

[2] Res enim fiscales quasi propriae et privatae principis sunt. Ulpian, *Digest*, lib. XLIII. tit. viii. 2, § 4.

[3] The similarity is borne out by the names of the imperial offices. It is instructive to compare the imperial officers of finance with their prototypes in private *familiae*. The term *procurator* was used for the slave in charge of a household, for the manager of a *dominus*, for a book-keeper.

care of the most distant provinces, while the roads which stretched through every part were the enduring channels through which both military and commercial intercourse was constantly maintained; they served as the outward and visible sign of the unity of a civilised world, conscious of its strength and proudly defiant of the chaos that lay beyond[1].

59. The parts of the Empire, into which Augustus was able to introduce his administrative system directly, were extensive; but before the time of Vespasian the range of direct imperial responsibility was still further increased, and embraced no fewer than twenty-five provinces. Egypt, Numidia and Mauritania in the south were his; so too were Syria, Judaea, and a larger part of Asia Minor. In the west Vespasian held the greater part of Spain, and Gaul, and Britain, while the northern part of the Empire along the whole length of the Danube valley was in his charge. The financial districts into which these regions were divided were administered by *procuratores*, who were personally accountable to the emperor himself, and who did not enjoy a brief period of practical irresponsibility as the Praetors had done under the Republic. Even in the provinces which remained formally under senatorial authority many important departments were controlled by imperial officials. The defence of the Italian coast and the maintenance of the public roads were in their hands; they too were responsible for the management of the public domain. Nor was the city of Rome exempt from their interference; they had to provide for the supply of corn, and for the introduction of water. Practical reforms followed the introduction of administrative change. The imperial judicial system was so effective that the worst abuses in the collection of taxes were checked, though the *publicani* continued to farm the customs[2], and some other branches of revenue. The sphere for speculators and contractors was gradually reduced, and in the

The sphere and method of imperial administration.

---

[1] Keary, *The Vikings in Western Christendom*, p. 1.
[2] Willems, *Droit Public Domain*, 498.

Second Century even the working of the mines was taken in hand by the State.

The problem of finding men for all these administrative posts could not have been easy at any time; it was doubly difficult in days when the standard of public morality was so remarkably low.   The great positions, like those of the legates, and still more the prefectures of the more important provinces and departments, were usually reserved for men of rank, and formed the prizes to which they might legitimately aspire; but the business of the Empire, like much of the business of households, was committed to freedmen.   The rise of this class into prominence is as characteristic of the early Empire, as the dominance of the *equites* had been of the late Republic; and for the same reason, since the work of financial administration was practically in the hands of each class in turn.   Augustus had conferred upon the freedmen a certain social status by opening up to wealthy individuals a field for the display of public spirit.   Under his successors they obtained prominent employment as *procuratores* or fiscal officers in all parts of the Empire, as well as in many other posts; and they were encouraged by the hope of promotion for good service, since some of them acted as heads of departments in the imperial palace itself.   The whole of the official correspondence, and of the business connected with the imperial revenue and with petitions to the Emperor, passed through the hands of freedmen in the time of Augustus[1].

The best guarantee for the good service of these officials lay, not in their character, but in the system of account which was devised[2].   Unfortunately the details which survive are few and meagre, but they suffice to show the character of the

[1] Hirschfeld, *Untersuchungen*, p. 32.

[2] The *procurator* in a household would submit his books for his master's approval: the imperial *procuratores* were in exactly the same relation to their imperial master, and the definite salary served to establish their position and to emphasize their responsibility.

system now introduced. By giving fixity to the demands of
the government, Augustus assured a measure of certainty to
the cultivator. The Ptolemaic system of finance had come
within measurable distance of that which was now introduced;
there was probably a survey of lands [1], and an estimate agreed
on between the cultivator and the contractor; in the Roman
census it appears that the account to be paid was not a fixed
proportion, but a fixed sum. This simplified the whole system
of collection, and gave a much greater security against arbitrary extortion. The first *census* of which we hear is that
which is mentioned in the Gospel of St Luke. It seems to
have included an enumeration of the population, and of the
taxable property [2]; the land belonging to public or private
owners was described not merely by measurement of its area,
but by estimates of its productive capabilities. A form of
survey has been preserved, which is at least as old as the time
of Trajan; it provides for the description of each estate according to the qualities of the soil for any purpose, and also
for the enumeration of the slaves and *coloni*. The *census*
returns taken in each district were preserved with care in the
archives of each province; but the ultimate authority in the
department lay with the Emperor himself at Rome [3]. The
census gave the basis for a sound calculation as to what
taxation, either of *lands* or *moveables*, a province would bear,
while it also afforded a means of detecting the extortionate
demands of officials if any complaint were made. Taxation
was at length placed on a sound basis, and was no longer dependent on the arbitrary power of irresponsible officers. Great
pains must also have been taken in making up an occasional
statement of the accounts of the Empire. This seems to have
been done habitually: Augustus was accustomed to have these

---

[1] See above, p. 129.

[2] The value of a rural district may often depend primarily on the number
of people available for tilling it. Cunningham, *Industry and Commerce*, I.
5, 170.   [3] Marquardt, II. 208.

statements published, and left a precise summary of the
financial condition of the empire at the time of his death [1].

These two great financial devices, a statistical survey, and
a regular reckoning with the officials, were the corner-stones of
good administration, and have been consciously or unconsciously adopted in the organisation of later realms. They
were the foundation of the fiscal system which was developed
in this country under the Norman kings. The *Liber Cen-
sualis* or Domesday Book of William is, in its form as well as
in its object, very closely illustrative of an imperial census [2];
while the organisation of the exchequer and the compilation of
the *Great Roll of the Pipe* must have had their analogy in the
official administration at Rome.

60.   The excellence of this administrative system enabled
the Roman Emperors to secure for their subjects
throughout the world the very boons, towards
which the policy of Rome had been directed,
while it was merely a little community threatened
by neighbouring tribes.   The old tradition still held good, and

The Cosmo-
politan State
and its insti-
tutions.

---

[1] Suet. *Aug.* 101 ; Willems, *op. cit.* 497.

[2] The form of the Roman Census, as taken in the time of Trajan, has
been preserved in the *Digest*, lib. L. tit. XV. de censibus 4.   It runs as follows : Forma censuali cavetur ut agri sic in censum referantur ; nomen fundi
cuiusque, et in qua civitate et quo pago sit, et quos duos vicinos proximos
habeat ; et id arvum, quod in decem annis proximis satum erit, quot
jugerum sit, vinea quot vites habeat ; olivetum quot jugerum et quot arbores
habeat ; pratum quod intra decem annos proximos factum erit, quot jugerum ;
pascua quot jugerum esse videantur ; item silvae caeduae ; omniaque ipse
qui defert aestimet.   The subsequent clauses about the taxation of those
who had land in more than one civitas, about beneficia immunitatis,
fisheries, harbours and salt-pans are of interest, as well as the directions to
note the nationality and employments of the slaves.   The points on which
William the Conqueror's commissioners were required to report were as
follows: Quomodo vocatur mansio ; quis tenuit eam tempore regis Edwardi ;
quis modo tenet ; quot hidae ; quot carrucae in dominio, quot hominum ;
quot villani, quot cotarii, quot servi, quot liberi homines, quot sochemani,
quantum silvae, quantum prati, quot pascuorum, quot moliendina, quot pis-
cinae.   *Inquisitio Eliensis* in *Domesday Book* III. 497.   The readjustments

constant attention was given to the frontiers in order to provide immunity from attack, while the planting of colonies and municipalities, and the liberal enfranchisement of provincials, diffused a condition of orderly government wherever the Roman power was felt.

By the time of Vespasian, when it was no longer necessary to conciliate the jealous interests and republican sentiments which had threatened Augustus at every step, considerable progress was made in bringing the forms of government to correspond more closely with existing fact. The Roman Republic had been the predominant partner in an Italian federation in which the individual character of each of the component parts was maintained, though they tended to approximate to the aristocratic type of constitution which the Roman people favoured so far as their allies were concerned. In imperial Rome these incongruous elements, with their distinctive features and separate histories and traditions, were preserved; but as the Empire came to be consolidated there was an increased homogeneity in its parts. The various outlying members, instead of being separately connected with the great city, came to be constituent parts of a larger whole; and similar classes, with similar status and living under the same laws, were found in every part.

The Flavian emperors pursued the old policy of securing the outlying districts of the Empire by founding colonies and planting cities. To the colonies groups of veterans were transferred and lands were allotted them; and the new municipalities enjoyed from the first the status and privileges of the Latin cities. The maintenance of good government in these communities was a matter of imperial concern; they were under occasional surveillance, and the frequent *rescripts*

of the land-revenue in the East every fifteen years, (Finlay, *History of Greece*, I. 219), were used as *indictions* for dating events in the West, and the tradition of the census must have been well known. On some traces of its survival in the West, see Cunningham, *Alien Immigrants*, p. 53.

of the Emperors on their affairs gradually assimilated diver-
gent customs and grew into a considerable body of municipal
law[1]. The older communities, overshadowed as they were by
the great expansion of Roman dominion[2], were no longer
jealous about preserving their ancient customs; and thus the
municipalities tended more and more to be shaped on a
common model[3].

One of the most important developments of this policy
appeared in the time of Alexander Severus. Though certain

[1] A very interesting example of imperial interference in what had once
been a municipal matter occurs in the edict of Diocletian (301 A.D.) which
was discovered at Stratonicaea (Eski-hissar) in Caria, and of which twenty-
one distinct examples are known. (Mommsen, *Corpus Inscriptionum
Latinarum*, III. 801, and Suppl. iii., 1909. K. Bücher, *Die Diokletianische
Taxordnung* in *Z. f. d. g. Staatswissenschaft*, L. (1894), p. 189.) It contains an elaborate list of the prices of products and goods, for the protection
of the public against the extortion of middlemen, and as a rate for pro-
visioning the army. The general dearness (or dearth) of the time, which
seems to be indicated by the existence of such an edict, may be taken as
one of the symptoms of the decay of the empire. There is no attempt to
fix prices, but only to lay down a limit for *maximum* prices. It has thus
little in common with the mediaeval attempts to settle *reasonable* prices,
or the system maintained by Elizabeth of assessing *reasonable* wages. The
principle of this edict in fixing a *maximum* rate for wares or wages, and
leaving the actual rate to be settled in some other fashion so long as the
maximum was not exceeded, is found in such measures as the Frankfort
Capitulare of 794, or in the *Statute of Labourers* and similar measures
adopted in different countries after the Black Death. Cunningham, *Growth
of Industry*, I. 333.

[2] The policy of local enfranchisement, inaugurated by Claudius, and
carried on by Galba, Otho, Vitellius, Vespasian and his successors, culminated in the notable edict of Caracalla (A.D. 211—217) in which he
conferred the *civitas* on all *Latini* and *peregrini* living under the sway of
Rome. He thus increased the area from which the legacy duty was drawn,
while he raised its rate from a twentieth to a tenth. Hitherto the privileges
of citizenship had counterbalanced its obligations in the provincial mind;
but now distinction disappeared in indiscriminate taxation—the new citizens
had everything to lose, and little or nothing to gain by their changed
position. Cf. Gibbon, book I. ch. 6; Willems, p. 398.

[3] Finlay, *History of Greece*, I. 111.

C. W. C.   12

ancient bodies had an established position[1], there had been frequent efforts in the later republican and early imperial times to put down unauthorised *collegia*[2]; but this emperor is said to have promoted the formation of these associations[3]. They were the instrument by which the regulation as well as the en-couragement of trade and industry in each centre was effected. As has been pointed out, they may have had their analogues in Greek towns, but it was under imperial control in the third century that they became public and authoritative institutions in the West. Their history in the early Middle Ages is obscure, and it may be difficult to prove direct historical continuity in particular places; but it is clear that the type which was so common in the third century had not been forgotten; when municipal life began to revive in the thirteenth century similar gilds and *corps-de-métier* everywhere sprang into being. Paris is commonly spoken of, though the evidence hardly seems conclusive, as a town where the old *collegia* survived all through the dark ages[4]; it was certainly one where they attained a great degree of vigour under St Louis.

There is some reason to believe that in rural districts also the cultivators enjoyed a somewhat better status than they had

---

[1] The institution of gilds of artisans is attributed to Numa, who is said, by Plutarch (*Numa*, c. 17), to have devised this means of breaking down the jealousy of Romans and Sabines, by organising the people on new lines. The gilds of musicians, goldsmiths, masons, dyers, shoemakers, tanners, braziers and potters are specified, and we are told that he "collected the other artificers also into companies, who had their respective halls, courts and religious ceremonies peculiar to each society." The terms in which it is mentioned preclude us from supposing that this institution was in any sense peculiar to Rome, and it is most unlikely that it was a native institution in that city (Dionys. Hal. *Antiq. Rom.* IX. 25). However, it obtained a firm hold in Rome in early times (*Digest*, lib. LVII. tit. XIX. 4), but there is no reason to suppose that the institution spread from this one centre to the Greek cities throughout the Empire.

[2] Suetonius, *Oct.* 32. Compare the careful discussion in Cohn, *Zum römischen Vereinsrecht*, 53 f.　　　[3] Lampridius, *Alex. Severus*, c. 33.

[4] Fagniez, *Études sur l'industrie à Paris*, 3.

done in republican times.   A considerable proportion of them
appear to have been tenant farmers, who were under no personal servitude, and were not exposed to the grinding misery
of the *ergastula*[1].   It seems not improbable that with the
cessation of conquest and the settlement of the more distant
provinces there was an increased difficulty in procuring slaves,
and that from their very scarcity they secured more favourable
treatment, while the position of the free labourer underwent
a corresponding improvement.   The legal position and general
condition of the *coloni* in the later Empire is unintelligible, except on the hypothesis that the cultivating peasantry had
enjoyed considerable prosperity in earlier times.

Such seems to have been the revival of industrial life both
in town and country during the two first centuries of our era.
Yet with all the improvement it is difficult to believe that
things were in a thoroughly healthy condition.   It is not easy
to point out the precise causes of material decay, for some
of the phenomena, which force themselves on our attention
even in the second and third centuries, must be regarded as
symptoms of a decadence that had already begun.   It is not
unlikely, as Meyer points out[2], that the secret of decay lay in
a loss of those political ideals and political enthusiasm which
had flourished in older days; the establishment of a world-
wide empire sapped the political interest of the cultured
classes[3], while the power of Caesar became the prey on which
military adventurers fixed their ambitions.

Some of the premonitory symptoms of decadence deserve
a passing notice.   There was, for one thing, an increase of
pauperism which attracted general attention.   Trajan instituted regular charitable funds, and there seems to have been

---

[1] Compare the description in Apuleius, *Metam.* IX. 12.   At the time of
the barbarian invasions the slaves occasionally rebelled against their masters.
Rocafort, *Paulinus de Pella*, 58.   Paulinus, *Eucharisticos*, 333.

[2] *Wirthschaftliche Entwickelung*, pp. 52, 54.

[3] Finlay, *op. cit.* I. 103.

a very large number of private benefactions for the same purpose[1]. It is true that the evidence furnished by statistics of pauperism is never conclusive; they may show that poverty was common in certain congested districts while other places were doing well, or perhaps that a serious attempt was made to relieve distress which had been callously ignored at other times. But there were other features of town life which are more difficult to explain away; the constant endeavour to overhaul municipal finance seems to show that it was badly managed, while the desire of prominent citizens to escape the burden of office is an unhealthy sign. The evidence as to the decline of the population[2] brings out a disastrous condition of affairs; under such peaceful conditions as the Empire afforded, one might have expected the population to increase with considerable rapidity. The fact that it seems to have declined certainly indicates that a lack of vigour affected all the peoples of the Roman Empire; whether this was due to physical or to moral causes, the vitality of the imperial subjects seems to have been so far sapped, that they did not make the most effective use of the centuries of peace, and were unprepared to resist the onslaught of the barbarians in the third century of our era.

[1] The reliefs were known as *alimenta, alimentationes,* and were under the care of special district officers (*quaestores, procuratores alimentorum,* &c.). Trajan obtained the necessary funds by lending money at a low rate on the security of landed estates belonging to members of the municipality concerned, and the interest was paid to the municipal chest for the orphans. Willems, p. 493. Caelia Macrina, in the time of the Antonines, left by her will sufficient property for the maintenance continually of 100 poor boys and girls, up to the ages of 16 and 19 respectively. The town of Veleia in Italy had a capital of 1,116,000 sesterces, devoted to similar purposes. Levasseur, I. p. 93. Hatch, *Bampton Lectures,* p. 34.

[2] Seeley, *Lectures and Addresses,* 48. That the emperors perceived the seriousness of this question is clearly seen from such enactments as the *Lex Julia et Papia Poppaea* (A.D. 18). Muirhead, *Historical Introduction to the Private Law of Rome,* p. 303. Houdoy, *Le droit municipal,* p. 501.

61. There were some sides from which the Roman Empire was in no danger of attack. The natural de-
fences, which had stood Egypt in such good   The difficulty
stead for centuries, protected the African do-   of defending
minions of Rome. The desert tribes could not assemble in   the Empire.
hordes so as to be a serious menace, and there were no
formidable armies to make their way across the sandy wastes.
The Mediterranean, which had come to be a Roman lake,
formed an inner line of defence so far as the heart of the
Empire was concerned; but there was real danger on the
northern and eastern frontiers. The rivers, which bounded
the Empire there, served as excellent lines of demarcation,
but not as barriers to restrain the hardy tribes, who were
nurtured in the plains and forests of Germany, or the peoples of the East, who had not forgotten the tradition of their
former greatness. The Marcomannic and Persian wars of the
third century were anticipatory waves of the tides of Teutonic
and Mohammedan invasion, which afterwards swept in turn
over the greater part of the Empire. Africa seemed to be
secure, but the Vandals found a road thither by way of
Spain; and the Mediterranean coasts were ravaged by pirate
fleets which were fitted out by the Goths at the mouth of
the Danube. It was from the north and east that danger
threatened, and it was in the north and east that an effective
system of military defence had to be maintained, since no
effective frontier had been provided by nature.

From the time of the Marcomannic war (A.D. 167—180)
an expedient was adopted, which seemed to promise well, of
planting semi-barbarian tribes within the limits of the Empire,
and thus providing a buffer against the wilder hordes beyond.
But this was in itself a confession of weakness; and in more
than one case the tribes, that were thus incorporated as Roman
soldiers, became conscious of their own strength, or rather
of the weakness of any forces that might be opposed to

them[1]. The settlement on the south side of the Danube was
the centre from which the Goths started on their career of
conquest.

But there was no method of defence which did not in-
volve danger. When a legion was planted in some outlying
district to keep guard on the frontier, they too felt that they
were in possession of power, and they were unwilling to
acknowledge a distant authority. In this way there came
to be a number of provincial emperors, who claimed and
maintained supreme authority in their own territory, like
Postumus in Gaul, or of tyrants who aspired to the Empire
of Rome and raised fruitless but disastrous rebellions. With
the beginning of the barbarian invasions and the consequent
concentration of power on the frontiers, the very evils, against
which Octavius had endeavoured to guard, reappeared. The
Empire was torn by dissension ; and the ingenious attempt of
Diocletian to place the supreme power in commission and
thus to maintain an effective control over the four quarters
of a united empire, did not serve as a remedy for the recurring
evils.

62. The most hasty survey of the Roman Empire, in the
third and fourth centuries, brings to light many
symptoms of decay. There were political disasters
and moral enervation, industrial stagnation and
commercial ruin. On the inner reasons for this
decadence and loss of vitality it is unnecessary
to speculate here, or to try to form a complete
diagnosis of the diseases from which the body politic suffered.
But when we look at the times from an economic standpoint, we
are at least in a position to see the interconnection between

*Deficient
supply of
money, and
consequent
difficulties in
the formation
of capital.*

---

[1] And the constant quarrels between actual or would be emperors
familiarised the adjacent barbarians with ideas of war and invasion on their
own account, and enabled them to seize their opportunity. De Broglie,
L'Église et l'Empire Romain au IVme Siècle, Pt. II. ch. v. 7.

various phenomena, and to take a convenient survey of the whole. We shall find too that the growth of many of the evils of the time is largely accounted for by the simple fact that the Empire was inadequately supplied with money.

In a civilization like that of Rome, where money economy is everywhere in vogue and the very existence of industry and agriculture depends on trade and the circulation of wares, funds of money, to serve as circulating capital[1], are an element on which material prosperity of every sort depends. When industry is carried on with the help of money[2], its fruits must be realised in money, and it is with money that new materials are procured. We know in the present day what distress may be caused in the commercial world, from the sudden raising of the Bank-rate and a difficulty in procuring money, or from variations in prices, due to changes in the value of money through the depreciation of silver or the appreciation of gold. Precisely similar inconveniences were felt in the ancient world in regard to prices; and there was this farther difficulty, that owing to the insufficient supply of bullion, it was not at all easy to hoard wealth or form new funds to replace capital as it was consumed.

The fiscal practice of the Empire, as it was systematised by Constantine, was to draw as much as possible of the circulating medium of the community "into the coffers of the state. No economy or industry could enable his subjects to accumulate wealth; while any accident, a fire, an inundation, an earthquake, or a hostile incursion of the barbarians, might leave a whole province incapable of paying its taxes, and plunge it in hopeless

---

[1] That portion of capital with which the employer pays for materials and services, till his outlay is replaced by the sale of finished goods.

[2] In primitive societies the case is entirely different: there each village is self-sufficing; barter of superfluities serves for commerce, and industrial or agricultural capital is represented by stock in trade; but where money economy is in vogue, capital is essential. Cunningham, *Modern Civilization*, 125.

debt and ruin[1]." The wealth thus ruthlessly collected was not wisely employed; much was expended in feeding the pauperised citizens, and providing them with spectacles; but even the money devoted to permanent improvement was often imprudently spent. Throughout the ancient world there was a constant tendency to sink accumulated wealth in palaces, temples and decorative buildings, rather than to employ it as capital for the production of wares. Though a large part of the imperial resources was devoted to public works, very little was employed on remunerative public works, i.e. on works which brought in an annual revenue and thus rendered it possible to replace the outlay expended upon them. Even the rapid sinking of capital in works which are ultimately remunerative may cause great commercial disaster, as it did at the time of the Railway mania; but many of the magnificent buildings of the ancients[2] had no pretences to be sources of revenue, and were costly to maintain. Harbours would of course often prove profitable investments; and the tolls collected at so many commercial barriers throughout the Empire[3] probably rendered the great military roads successful as commercial undertakings. Still it seems probable that a very large proportion of the wealth, both of the Empire and of the municipalities within it, was sunk unremuneratively. One town had vied with another in magnificence, and serious disaster overtook them when the Empire was reorganised, and when Diocletian diverted the resources of the local treasuries[4] to pay the salaries of new officials, and to give donatives to the legions. There is reason to believe that the strictly reproductive expenditure in the

[1] Finlay, *Greece*, I. 106.

[2] On the large expenditure on buildings under Diocletian compare Lactantius, *De mort. persecut.* 7.

[3] Cagnat, *Impôts indirects chez les Romains*, 19.

[4] Gibbon, *Decline and Fall*, c. xiii. Alexander Severus had pursued the opposite policy of aiding local resources by making large grants for the rebuilding of provincial cities. Lampridius, c. 44.

maintenance of roads and bridges was gradually curtailed[1]. Wherever we look, we see that there was a continual drain of capital by the State; at best it was sunk, at worst it was wasted, but it was not utilised in a fashion in which it could be easily replaced.

This might have been of comparatively little importance if there had been much opportunity for the saving of wealth and the formation of fresh capital; but this was not the case. Capital cannot be formed unless there are supplies of a material available for hoarding. In the present day, owing to credit and the facilities for banking, this is less strictly true; but in the Roman Empire, bullion was practically the sole material available for hoarding, and therefore for the accumulation of capital: and the precious metals were not at all plentiful. In the first century of the Christian era there was a very large export of silver to China, India and Arabia[2]; though it is possible that the demand for incense declined in the fourth century, yet silk—which was worth its weight in gold—continued to be much sought after; and it seems highly improbable that the drain of silver to the East[3], which continued during the Middle Ages, was suspended at any period of the history of the Empire, or was counteracted by large supplies from the mines of Spain. The frightful debasement of the currency, by which emperor after emperor tried to obtain the means of paying his troops, is additional evidence of the scarcity of bullion; while it must have aggravated commercial risks by the uncertainty it introduced into trade. "The depreciation in the value of the circulating medium during the fifty years between the reign of Caracalla and the death of Gallienus annihilated a great part

[1] A great deal of Hadrian's outlay was devoted to roads and remunerative works (Finlay, 1. 65), but after his time they were neglected (*Ib.* 1. 77). Hodgkin, *Italy and her Invaders*, II. 581.

[2] Pliny, *Nat. Hist.* XII. 18 (41).

[3] Large payments had also to be made from time to time to the barbarian invaders for the redemption of captives. Laurentius, *De magistratibus*, III. 75.

of the trading capital in the Roman Empire, and rendered it impossible to carry on commercial transactions, not only with foreign countries, but even with distant provinces[1]." Among other evils it would increase rather than diminish the drain on the small stock of precious metals[2].

These conditions rendered it exceedingly difficult for any-one to save wealth; they also made men unwilling to risk their accumulations in business of any kind, and to use it as capital. The complete uncertainty in regard to prices paralysed trade, and capitalists were "induced to hoard their coins of pure gold and silver for better days[3]," which never came. Industry did not offer a tempting field, as the enterprising man of business would often have to face the competition of a manufactory organised by the State, and controlled by officials whom it would be imprudent to offend[4]. There was even greater disinclination to use capital in agriculture and apply it to permanent improvements. This was partly due to the rights which tenants[5] could acquire, and which interfered with proprietary control; it called forth the measures which prevented proprietors from diverting their slaves from agricultural labour[6]. Accumulated

[1] Finlay, *Hist. of Greece*, I. 52.

[2] There were strict limits as to the amounts of money which merchants might carry for their expenses, and severe punishment for the export of bullion (*Cod. Theo.* lib. IX. tit. 23, 1) much as at a later time in Spain. But the policy pursued was bullionist and not mercantilist. See Cunningham, *Growth of Industry*, II. 211.

[3] Finlay, I. 52. It also appears, from the edict of Diocletian (Wadding-ton's edition, p. 7, l. 51), that the government failed to realise the advantage which would accrue to the Empire generally from encouraging commercial intercourse. It was one of his objects, in fixing a maximum price, to prevent middlemen from engrossing goods in one district in order to transport them to a place where high prices might be obtained. Where there was a tariff throughout the Empire there would be less opportunity for profitable commerce between distant places. On similar regulations in the Gothic kingdom compare Finlay, I. 267.

[4] Finlay, I. 117.

[5] Finlay, I. 154. *Corpus Juris Civilis, Cod.* XI. tit. 48. 2. and 19.

[6] Finlay, I. 200.

wealth was hoarded rather than invested, and general decay
ensued; money and circulating capital are not necessary for
the maintenance of human life[1], but they were necessary for
the maintenance of a civilized society like the Roman Empire.
Since capital was not available, there need be no surprise
that labour failed to find employment and that land went out
of cultivation; these again are the very circumstances in which
population would necessarily decline.

63.   The scarcity of bullion, together with the difficulties
in regard to the accumulation and investment of
capital, had a natural result, as it gave moneyed   Usury and
men the advantage of a monopoly[2].   There is   the collection
                                                  of revenue.
abundant evidence that in the third and fourth
centuries the evils of usury reappeared on a large scale[3].
The agriculturists and industrial classes alike required the
command of money to pay the taxes ; and many of them must
have been compelled to have recourse to usurers in order to
meet the demands of the State.   The *aurum negotiatorium*
was a tax levied on all those who were engaged in dealings
of any kind, except day labourers and cultivators who sold the
products of their own land[4].   It was levied every fifth year in

[1] Adam Smith's criticism of mercantilism was sound for his own time ;
but it is none the less true that the policy which the mercantilists advo-
cated has been unduly depreciated.   Bullion is necessary in many societies
in order to form *treasure*, for political purposes—and *capital* for industry
and commerce; and the mercantilists of the seventeenth century, with their
doctrine of the balance of trades, were trying to afford conditions for the
accumulation of these two—treasure and capital.   The Roman Empire had
neither of them, and it perished.

[2] The moneyers showed themselves a very powerful corporation, under
Aurelian.   Finlay, I. 52.

[3] Lampridius, *Alex. Severus*, cc. 21, 26.   This is apparent from the
language of the Fathers, e.g. St Ambrose, *De Tobia*, St Chrysostom,
Homily lvi. on St Matthew xvii. and St Augustine on Psalm xxxvi. 26.
The Apostolical Canons (c. 6) forbid the clergy to lend for usury, and the
prohibition was extended to the laity in the Canons of Elvira (c. 20).

[4] *Cod. Theo.* lib. XIII. tit. 1, 12.   Lampridius, *Alex. Sever.* 24.   Levasseur, *Classes ouvrières*, I. 74.

the time of Constantine, and for many of those who were assessed, it was quite impossible to make up their quota of payment[1] from their own resources. The taxpayers' necessities were the usurers' opportunities.

As wealth decreased the burden of taxation became relatively heavier, and there was much hardship in connection with the collection of revenue. Lactantius gives a most miserable picture of the severities that were inflicted under the guise of penalties for endeavouring to escape the taxes. "Slaves were dealt with to accuse their masters, and wives to accuse their husbands; when no sort of evidence could be found, men were forced by torture to accuse themselves....After that all men were thus listed, then so much money was laid upon every man's head, as if he had been to pay so much for his life. Yet this matter was not trusted to the first taxmen, but new sets of them, one after another, were sent about; that new men might always find new matter to work upon; and though they could really discover nothing, yet they increased the numbers in the lists that they made, that so it might not be said they had been sent to no purpose. By the means of those oppressions, the stock of the cattle was much diminished, and many men died; and yet the taxes continued still to be levied, even for those that were dead; to such misery were men reduced, that even death did not put an end to it[2]."

It would be a mistake, however, to suppose that the moneyed men, who advanced money on usury and farmed the taxes, had an easy time of it. Their position corresponded with that of the Jews in Angevin England; they were the instruments of oppression, but they were mercilessly squeezed themselves. They appeared to prosper at the expense of their neighbours, and there was no scruple in taxing them heavily. The *aurum coronarium*[3] was imposed upon them, and the

---

[1] Zosimus, II. 449.

[2] Lactantius, *De mort. persecut.* 23 (Burnet).

[3] Hodgkin, *Italy*, II. 603.

succession duties would hit them very heavily. Public opinion
at the time was inclined to regard all commercial gain with
suspicion[1], and to treat all usurers and middlemen as rascals
whom it was fair to pillage when opportunity arose. There
was a constant "war against private wealth," especially when
its owners failed in the primary public duty of collecting the
allotted revenue[2].

64. The pressure of public burdens appears to have been
one of the principal reasons for the changes in
the structure of society which were taking place   Loss of
at this time. The duties of an official, instead   economic
                                                       freedom.
of affording opportunities for gain, entailed
onerous responsibilities, and it became necessary to compel
men to undertake them. The galling character of the restrictions, which were gradually laid upon the decurions, comes out
in the laws of the Theodosian Code[3], nearly two hundred in
number, which are devoted to the subject. The son of a
decurion was bound to the curia ; and he was prevented from
entering any calling—such as the army or the church—which
might interfere with the discharge of his curial obligations.
Indeed all economic freedom was at an end so far as the most
honoured classes within the Empire were concerned; even
freedom of movement was prohibited. The decurions were
"forbidden to take any kind of journey lest they should de-
fraud the curia of their services, and for the same reason they
were forbidden to leave the cities and take up their residence
in the country[4]."

There was a similar loss of personal independence among
the artisan classes ; though in their case it was connected with

[1] Naudet, *Changements dans l'administration de l'empire romain*,
II. 119. On the plausibility of the widely current opinion that merchants'
gain arises by successful cheating see Cunningham, *Modern Civilization*,
24 n.

[2] Finlay, I. 220.

[3] Lib. XII. tit. I.

[4] Hodgkin, *Italy*, II. 585. *Cod. Theo.* lib. XII. tit. I. cc. 18, 143, 144.

responsibility for contributing to the taxes, rather than with responsibility for exercising office. The *collegia* had ceased to be regarded as dangerous associations uncontrolled by the State; they came to be used as instruments for retaining a hold on the taxpayer. Their responsible members were in all probability small capitalists[1], rather than mere wage-earners, as in the mediaeval organisation of labour. The imposition of the *aurum negotiatorium* under Alexander Severus became a reason for keeping the workman and the shopkeeper under strict surveillance, so that he might not escape the tax which was levied every fifth year. They were unable to leave their city, or to hold aloof from the *collegium*; the *Zunftzwang* was enforced in most stringent fashion. Libanius[2] describes the misery caused by the attempts to exact money from poor men, who were quite unable to pay a relatively large sum to the tax-collector even at long intervals; a similar sum collected more frequently would have been far less ruinous. But the strictly stereotyped system of labour organisation[3], which the collection of revenue entailed, was in itself a serious hindrance to industrial enterprise or progress.

Changes of a similar character had already taken place in the management of land. It seems to be clear that the *colonus*, as we hear of him in the first century of our era, was economically free; he appears to have hired land for stated periods, and to have been free to leave it when his time expired[4]; and as he paid his rent in money he was personally independent. From this position he seems to have fallen into

[1] 'Merchants' in the sense in which the name applies to the members of a Gild Merchant. *Growth of Industry and Commerce*, I. 221.

[2] Naudet, *op. cit.* 218. On the rejoicing over the remission of this tax in 498 A.D. see *The Chronicle of Joshua the Stylite*, c. 31.

[3] This survived at Constantinople in the time of Leo VI. and is clearly described in τὸ ἐπαρχικὸν βιβλίον. Prof. Nicole sees in this over-organisation one of the causes of the ultimate fall of the Eastern Empire. *Livre du préfet*, 7.

[4] Fustel de Coulanges' *Recherches*, p. 67 f.

the condition of a serf, who had become permanently attached to the soil, and paid his rent in labour and kind; nor are indications wanting that it was through a burden of indebtedness[1] that the peasant lost his freedom so completely. Estates were valued for fiscal purposes according to the head of labour they possessed, and the interest of the Roman proprietor would generally be to reinstate a defaulting tenant as a caretaker, rather than to evict him[2]. Here once more we see how the pressure of public burdens, at a time when material prosperity was decaying, contributed to the loss of economic freedom.

With the decay of private enterprise, both in town and country districts, it became necessary for the State to make increased efforts to organise industrial undertakings. This was especially necessary in order to secure a sufficient food supply in Rome, and in the larger towns of the provinces, and the *navicularii* and *pistores* were so organised as to be practically departments of state[3], while many forms of manufacturing industry were carried on in state workshops and factories. They were principally intended to supply arms and munitions of war, but they were also organised in order to furnish articles of luxury for the imperial palace. The labour was partly that of slaves and criminals, as well as of freedmen; but there were besides a certain number of free labourers who were glad to take engagements in these factories. Raw materials were supplied to each workshop and had to be carefully accounted for; the proportion of the products to be paid to the Emperor, and the amount of work to be done by the various labourers, were strictly and stringently defined. Though slavery had greatly declined—partly in all probability from the increasing difficulty in procuring a regular supply of slaves—the

---

[1] That this was directly or indirectly due to the pressure of taxation is highly probable. Salvianus, *De gub. Dei*, v. 7. 8. Amm. Marcellinus, XVI. 5. *Chronicle of Joshua the Stylite*, c. 39.

[2] Finlay, I. 153.

[3] Levasseur, I. 46.

free labourer had everywhere lost his economic freedom and was reduced to practical servitude and personal dependence. The steps in retrogression correspond closely to the steps in progress that have been described above[1]; the insufficient supply of money, and gradual reversion to a natural economy, involved the loss of economic freedom, and when this was done away, political freedom was no longer possible.

The ruin of the provinces in republican times had been due to the operations of private capitalists; in the Roman Empire it was at least accelerated and accentuated by the pressure of public burdens. Formerly the lack of administration had been an evil, but the pressure of an expensive, excessive, and, as it became, an inefficient administration wrought very similar havoc at a later time. The old evils appeared under new conditions; the misery in imperial times was not so much due to external circumstances, as to the decay of the vigorous spirit which could strive to cope with them[2].

It has been pointed out above how the introduction of money-economy, despite its disadvantages, gave the opportunity in Greek cities for individual citizens to take part in free political life, with all its duties including that of military service. But under the Roman Empire, maintained by a large standing army[3], there was no real field for the legitimate ambitions of the law-abiding citizen[4]; a general might lead a successful revolution, but there was little of a career for the non-official classes. The loss of vigour may be partly ascribed to the very effectiveness of the administration, which led the people to

---

[1] See above, p. 94.

[2] For a curious portrait of a Gallo-Roman noble and his occupations compare the *Eucharisticos* of Paulinus of Pella, 187 sq. in *Corpus Script. Eccl.* XVI. p. 198.

[3] Seeley, *Lectures and Addresses*, p. 17.

[4] In so far as Socialism closes fields of legitimate individual ambition it is in danger of reproducing the evils under which the Roman Empire fell; it is not easy to see what safeguards it could provide against them.

depend on Caesar for all the affairs of daily life and helped to impair a spirit of municipal self-help. They lost their interest in public life; men had outlived the old inspirations and enthusiasms, and none had taken their place as motives of individual effort or the will to live.

Other circumstances exercised an injurious influence on the spirit of the age. It is difficult to say how far the infusion of oriental luxury caused a real deterioration in the masses of the population; it is at least unproved that this was a potent factor, but the pressure of public burdens was an increasing disability that ate the very heart out of the capitalist and the labourer alike: there was no hope to inspire energy or encourage enterprise, and the gradual decay culminated in an utter collapse. The revival came at last, but only after centuries of misery; and when Christendom arose, the renascence of civilization was due to new influences and was effected by institutions distinct in character from those that had played the chief part in the old life.

65. Such seem to have been the principal economic reasons for the decay of the Empire; it is un- *The ruin of* necessary to dwell on the ulterior effects. The *the West.* defence of the realm hopelessly failed, and no effort was made to maintain an effective military organisation, at all events in the outlying provinces. The regular routine of justice was no longer observed, and the very tradition of the Civil Law died out over large areas of Europe where it had once been actively administered. The religion, which had come to be publicly adopted, was completely swept away in Britain, as well as the more primitive faiths which Christianity had superseded. In several of the provinces the language of the Empire ceased to hold its own. The fiscal system utterly broke down, and the various departments of government could not continue in efficiency with no visible means of support.

There were, indeed, in Gaul, Spain and Italy at all events, some municipal communities which survived the storm and

maintained the tradition of Roman civilization. But they
were few and far between. The cities of Britain seem to
have ceased to exist as centres of social life[1], and over large
areas of Northern France and Southern Germany, Roman
traditions had but a feeble influence, if they continued at
all. Some of these towns were dependent for their prosperity on commerce; they had been depots where goods
were collected for interchange, or where corn was shipped
for Rome. The interruption of commerce was fatal to their
very existence; or, if they had been centres of industry, there
were no opportunities for procuring materials or disposing of
the products of their labours. The economic basis of their
life was destroyed, or at best only served to maintain a greatly
diminished population.

In some of the rural districts the destruction was also
complete; the villas were unoccupied, and the areas which
had once been well tilled were overgrown with forest or
passed back into mere prairie. The remains of the houses
and mills turn up at times, as well as the stones which mark
the boundaries of the estates; they are relics which show
how important the civilization, which has since been completely
destroyed, had formerly been. The Roman lines of communication, and the cereals and trees and animals they introduced,
are the most permanent records of their influence on agriculture[2].
It might seem strange that such destruction could occur; but
we may remember that, after all, the food supply of any district is easily exhausted. If stock and seed-corn are left to
the cultivators, they may manage to pull through, with pri-
vation indeed, yet still effectually; but when a ruthless soldiery
plunder and destroy what they cannot carry away, there is no
possibility of recommencing tillage. The necessary means
are wanting. The wretched inhabitants may take to hunting
or fishing, they may drag on a miserable existence in caves

[1] G. G. Chisholm in *Geographical Journal* (Nov. 1897), X. 512.
[2] Cf. Gibbon, I. ch. ii.

or woods, but they cannot start their agriculture afresh without outside help.

For all that, it is probably true to say that from no province which once formed part of the Roman Empire have the deeply branded marks of her dominion been altogether obliterated; material relics at least bear witness to show what once was there. In other territories there were civic communities which preserved not only material objects, but social institutions and industrial arts such as had been practised in the Roman Empire. How much or how little was preserved in any given province is an archaeological problem of much interest. Elements survived in many places, which were incorporated as a new society was gradually upraised, but centuries elapsed before Western Europe recovered the prosperity and refinement which it had enjoyed in the time of Hadrian.

CHAPTER IV.

CONSTANTINOPLE.

66. THE story of the city, which Constantine refounded and made the capital of the East, contrasts curiously with that of the ancient capital at Rome and the Western portion of the Empire. Constantinople presented a bulwark which successfully resisted the shocks that shattered classical civilization to pieces in Italy, Gaul and Spain. Its strength and persistence is one of its chief marvels; but just because it lasted so long and made such effective resistance to the Barbarians and the Mohammedans, we are able to observe more clearly the nature of the evils before which the Eastern Empire eventually succumbed. The history of Constantinople is instructive, in so far as it can be contrasted with that of Rome, and equally instructive where similarities can be traced between them.

Old and New Rome contrasted.

The most striking contrast is in the physical situation of the new Rome. It has been pointed out, in a preceding section, that the difficulty of defending the long stretch of land frontier, which could only be reached by land routes, was a constant strain on the military resources of the Empire. The task of effective administration was difficult; and Rome was so situated as to be an inconvenient centre for government. When the Empire was reorganised under Diocletian it ceased to be the sole administrative centre, as it had to yield its place to four cities where the resources of each prefecture could be massed for the defence of the northern frontier—Nicomedia, Sirmium, Milan and Treves. When the

Empire was reunited under Constantine, he did not revert to the old capital, but sought out a new one; and he found the situation which suited his purpose in the ancient Greek colony of Byzantium.

Rome had, from its earliest days, expanded as a territorial power, and its position had been central and convenient for controlling a territory like the Italian peninsula; but it had no harbour, and no direct access to the sea. Byzantium was not only a position of great natural strength, as Constantine found when he set himself to wrest it from Licinius; it was also a maritime town, which had been selected by the men of Megaris as an admirable depot for trade between the Euxine and the Aegean. Its position on the sea rendered the food supply far more secure than that of Rome had ever been, as it could draw both from Egypt and the north of the Euxine; and it was a centre from which it was easy to communicate with the more important provinces by sea. The success of Justinian in overthrowing the Vandal Kingdoms in Africa, in securing Sicily, in contesting Italy with the Goths and obtaining a footing in Spain, serve to demonstrate 'the influence of sea power'; and Constantinople was an arsenal from which the 'sovereignty of the sea' could be conveniently maintained.

The physical strength of Constantinople, both from its position and its communications, is demonstrated by the magnificent manner in which it held its own, as the protector of all that was left of ancient civilization for more than a thousand years. As each century came, a new horde of invaders appeared. In the fourth century, immediately after its foundation, it was threatened by the Goths; in the fifth, by Huns and Vandals; in the sixth, by Slavs; these were succeeded by Arabs and Persians in the seventh, and Magyars, Bulgars and Russians in the eighth and ninth. Even after its prestige had been broken by the success of Venice and the Fourth Crusade, and the establishment of a Latin

Kingdom, the restored empire was able to maintain a long resistance against the Turks. It had often been shaken, but not till 1453 did it utterly succumb; it bore the brunt of the attacks of barbarism on Imperial civilization for a thousand years after Rome was pillaged by the Goths (A.D. 410) and Romulus Augustus ceased to reign (A.D. 476).

A brief consideration of this striking fact enables us to distinguish the precise service which the new Rome has rendered to Western Civilization. The old Rome diffused throughout the immense area of the Empire the arts of peace and of government; the new Rome preserved them unimpaired, so that, as order was gradually restored in Spain and Italy, in France and England, the new peoples might recover what their forefathers had destroyed when they devastated the Roman provinces. The new Rome retained in a limited area the best of that civilization which the old Rome had disseminated through the regions it conquered. The revival of civilized life in the West had in many ways a new and special character of its own, and it embodied some of the surviving fragments and local relics of Imperial civilization; but it was also affected in a remarkable degree by the indirect influence which was exercised, through many channels, by the Empire as it was maintained at Constantinople.

67. There are few more interesting tasks in any branch of social study than to consider the operation of similar causes under slightly different circumstances. In the case of the Eastern provinces we have several historians who describe in detail the effects which resulted from war, pestilence and oppressive government, under their very eyes; we know that similar visitations occurred in the West, and we can easily draw the parallel for ourselves, though no writer has chronicled in such detail the influence of each separate mischief there[1].

Similarities in their conditions.

[1] There is a graphic summary in the *Poema Conjugis* (17 *seq.*) attributed to Prosper of Aquitaine; see also Salvian, *De gub. Dei.*

It is in the story of the East, and in histories written in the East, that we come to understand what the ravages of war really meant. The Goths, insulted and cheated, left Moesia to ravage the plains that lay open to them, and crossing the Balkans, annihilated the legions of Valens at Hadrianople in 378 A.D. The story of the destruction they wrought[1] is at least an illustration of the similar attacks of Alaric on Italy, and of the Vandals on Africa. The wars of Belisarius, in the service of Justinian, give some idea of the utter desolation which must have overtaken the countries where these desperate struggles were repeatedly waged[2]; and the destruction of Antioch by the Persians exemplified the fate of other Roman cities[3].

There are occasional mentions of pestilence in other lands[4]; it was only too likely to break out in the course of sieges and in the neighbourhood of battle-fields[5]. But one visitation has been described as it occurred at Constantinople in 542 A.D., when, as is reported, no fewer than 5,000 persons perished daily. More than a century elapsed before England, with its vigorous population frequently recruited from without, recovered from the loss caused by the Black Death; and the plague at Constantinople seems to have been similarly disastrous, while no real recuperative forces were at work. In many houses every single inhabitant was carried off, and business of every kind was suspended for a time. Those who were affected by it and recovered, had their vitality strangely sapped by the illness; Justinian never regained his old vigour,

---

[1] The Gothic mercenaries in the East were a constant scourge to the population they protected. *Chronicle of Joshua the Stylite*, cc. 93—96.

[2] On the ravages round Edessa, see the *Chronicle of Joshua the Stylite*, cc. 52, 75.

[3] Bury, *Later Roman Empire*, I. 423.

[4] *Chronicle of Joshua the Stylite*, c. 41.

[5] *Ib.* cc. 53, 85.

and the whole effectiveness of the administration seemed to be diminished[1].

In the East, too, we see the effects of over-administration[2]; the army and the civil service were entirely distinct in their traditions and organization, and this distinction became more marked as the barbarian elements in the army grew larger and larger, and barbarian generals attained supreme commands. The professionalism of the army was as marked as the officialism of the bureaucratic administrators: every civil post throughout the Empire was filled by men with little local knowledge or sympathy, but with proper official training. The severance of these two departments from one another and from the ordinary population was a real evil; in regard to the civilians it probably increased the mischiefs which were due to oppressive taxation[3]. In the time of Justinian, the naval and military expenses were enormous, but he also made an extraordinary outlay in buildings of many kinds[4]. Churches, like St Sophia at Constantinople and Santo Apollinare-in-Classe near Ravenna, testify to the skill of his architects and the lavishness of his taste; and he also built numerous fortresses in different parts of the Empire. The military expenditure together with the outlay on unremunerative public works which has been already commented upon, reappears in

---

[1] Procopius, *Bell. Pers.* II. cc. 22, 23, 30. Bury, *Later Roman Empire*, I. 402.

[2] Other causes which have been already alluded to as combining to sap the vigour of the Roman Empire were also working with increased force after the time of Constantine, e.g. the pauperisation by doles of food. Hodgkin, *Italy and her Invaders*, II. 590.

[3] On the administrative changes introduced by Diocletian and Constantine and the increased economic burden they caused, see De Broglie, *L'Église et l'Empire Romain au IVme Siècle*, I. ii. pp. 195 and 235.

[4] For an account of Justinian's buildings and restorations in Constantinople, Mesopotamia, Armenia, Europe, Asia Minor, Palestine, N. Africa, see Procopius *de Aedificiis*, translated by Aubrey Stewart for the *Palestine Pilgrims' Text Society*. (1886.)

his time. Even when such works were superintended by a man
of his indomitable activity, the cost was enormous[1], and the
fiscal expedients to which he had recourse were exhausting to
the Empire.

68. The history of the Eastern Empire at the time of its
greatest extent, and when its most magnificent
public works were on hand, also seems to illustrate what has been said above on the decay
of vigour in the citizen population throughout the Empire.
The "Greens" and "Blues" of the Circus were not deficient
in intellectual activity, and the factions displayed an amount
of courage which compares favourably with the character of
the mob of Rome; but they seem to have been wanting in
that stability of purpose and in that enterprise which are
necessary to carry through any great undertakings. That
this was true of the army and its generals we know; but
the same defect is illustrated in the story of the commerce
of the time.

The Greek population and commerce.

Justinian was fully alive to the importance of trade, and
especially of intercourse with the East; it was the means
of procuring silk and other articles of luxury, and it also
afforded a substantial revenue, which must if possible be increased. Hence, the care for commerce is one of the most
important features of his reign, and mercantile considerations
appear to have affected a great deal of his foreign policy. His
conquest of the barbarian kingdoms gave the opportunity
for a revival of trade in the Western Mediterranean[2].

His *commerciarii* served a double purpose, at least at the
depots of Eastern trade[3]; they were not only concerned in

---

[1] There is abundant evidence of very severe fiscal pressure, though it
is not clear that Justinian was aware of the expedients adopted by his
officials. Bury, I. 336, 353.

[2] Finlay, I. 267.

[3] The trade had been carried on at recognised fairs, like that at Batnae,
near the Euphrates (Amm. Marcel. XIV. 3; *Corpus Juris Civilis*, Cod.
IV. tit. 63, 4).

the collection of customs, but also acted as imperial agents with exclusive rights for the purchase of raw silk from the barbarians[1]. At Constantinople the manufacture of this product was organised on a considerable scale in the *gynaecea* of the palace under the charge of the *comes largitionum*, and a great deal of effort was directed to keeping open the routes by which it was transferred. The inner reason of the antagonism between Persia and the Empire was connected with this traffic[2]; the frequent wars were not wholly due to national sentiments or personal ambitions; these doubtless were operative, but struggles become more intelligible when we see what each party had to gain. The Persians, in the time of Justinian, commanded the whole territory between the Caspian Sea and the Persian Gulf, and exacted heavy tolls; Justinian endeavoured by agreement with the Ethiopians[3] to open up a maritime trade with the mouths of the Indus, and thus procure silk from Ceylon or other stations which Chinese ships frequented; while he also tried to form Turkish connections so as to organise mercantile intercourse along a northern route, for which the independent city of Cherson formed a depot[4]. In each case commerce and war were closely connected. The fundamental objects aimed at in the wars with Persia were the possession of Nisibis in Mesopotamia and access to the Euphrates and Persian Gulf; the Persians, in defence of their monopoly, controlled the harbours at the Indus and spoiled the Ethiopians' market, while the commercial connections with the Turks may have done something to fire their ambitions and attract them westward.

---

[1] Zachariae von Lingenthal, *Eine Verordnung Justinians über den Seidenhandel* in *Mem. de l'Acad. de S. Pétersbourg*, Série VII. t. IX. No. 6, p. 9. Compare also *Corpus Juris Civilis, Cod.* IV. tit. 40, 2.

[2] Bury, I. p. 472.

[3] Jotaba came to be the important depot on this line of trade. Bury, I. 231, 295.

[4] Finlay, I. 144, 251.

The difficulties connected with the import of silk led Justinian to adopt an obvious expedient, and to try to introduce sericulture within the area of the Empire. Pains were taken to cultivate the mulberry in Greece, but a more important development occurred in Syria. This province was one of the most flourishing regions of the Eastern Empire, and the revival of its agriculture, industry and commerce recalled the great period of Phœnician prosperity. Not only did the Syrians throw themselves with energy into these new lines of enterprise, but they seem to have been the principal agents in carrying on the trade in different parts of the Levant. The Syrian and the Jew[1] were at least as active as the Greek in different branches of shipping between Constantinople and Egypt, and even between Constantinople and the towns on the Western Mediterranean. The Greeks may have monopolised the official posts, but the Semites seem to have been to the front in every sphere where private enterprise was essential.

Since they took so little part in commercial enterprise within the Empire it seems that the Greeks of Justinian's time were no longer the free and vigorous people who had gradually ousted the Phœnicians from the Mediterranean trade, and had planted their own colonies on the coasts of the Black Sea and of Africa. The change becomes more striking when we notice

[1] In the sixth century the Jewish nation attained a new importance; Finlay accounts for their increase in numbers and success in business by saying that the decay of civilization and oppression of other classes made a relative improvement in the position of the Jews, whose condition had previously been as bad as possible. The Jews too "were the only neutral nation who could carry on their trade equally with the Persians, Ethiopians, Arabs and Goths; for though they were hated everywhere, the universal dislike was a reason for tolerating a people never likely to form a common cause with any other." They had already risen to considerable importance in Gaul, Italy and Spain; and they were patronised by Theodoric and other barbarian kings, who found they were enabled to remain independent of Greek commerce. Finlay, I. 270.

that the opening up of distant trade was attempted by arrangements with neighbouring peoples, and not by the personal
energy of Greek adventurers. They trusted to the Turks[1]
as their agents in communication with China by the northern
route, and to the Ethiopians for the same friendly office in the
southern waters. With regard to another, if less important, line
of distant commerce, the same thing holds good. There is no
evidence of Greeks forcing their way to the Baltic lands to
purchase furs and amber; but there is ample reason to believe
that the kinsmen of the Goths habitually visited Constantinople.
How early this intercourse[2] began it is not easy to say. It was
certainly of importance in the ninth century; but the matter of
interest for us lies in the fact that it was mainly carried on through
the agency of Northmen who visited Constantinople, not of
Greeks who found their way to the Baltic. The Greeks in fact
had lost their preeminence in commerce, and were content to
look on idly while others reaped the profits of active trade.

69. There was indeed an excuse for the Greeks of Con-

The Station-
ary State.
stantinople, if they were so well content with
their own city and the life they enjoyed in it, as
to be unwilling to spend their days as pioneers in barbarous
lands. Their civilization in a great city, which was the heart
of a great Empire, was the most complete the world had ever

[1] A numerous colony of inhabitants of Central Asia was established at
Constantinople in the reign of Justin II. Finlay, *History of Greece*, I.
p. 267 *seq.* "Six hundred Turks availed themselves at one time of the
security offered by the journey of a Roman ambassador to the Great Khan
of the Turks and joined his train. This fact affords the strongest evidence
of the great importance of this route (to India), as there can be no question
that the great number of the inhabitants of Central Asia who visited
Constantinople were attracted to it by their commercial occupations."

[2] The evidence of coins seems to show that there was a great deal of
trade between the Baltic and some districts of the Empire in the early part
of the third century, Du Chaillu, *Viking Age*, II. 536, and that this subsequently declined. Similar evidence proves the existence of an active
trade with Arabia, and presumably through Constantinople, in the ninth
century. Montelius, *Civilization of Sweden*, 125.

seen; they had a heritage to guard, but had little incentive
to aim at farther progress[1].   All the triumphs of the past in
the development of human skill and the organisation of human
society, were at their service.

The fertile plains which lay within easy reach were cultivated
to a high pitch of perfection.   The best methods of working
and managing land had been considered by Greek citizens like
Xenophon, and the art had been perfected by Carthaginians
and Romans.   On their villas all this knowledge could be
brought to bear, while they were trying to cultivate new kinds
of products which reached them from the far East.

As a city too, Constantinople was one of the noblest the
world had ever seen.   Constantine laid out the capital on
an unprecedented scale, and its streets were crowded with
a busy population.   The inhabitants had but little political
freedom, but they were no mere slaves, leading a life of
unintelligent drudgery.   Without free institutions, they yet
engaged in keen intellectual debate, and vigorous partisanship
was a substitute for public opinion[2]; they enjoyed something
of that city life which the Greeks had developed; while their
skill in all industrial occupations is testified by the glories that
yet remain to St Sophia[3].

Though the best that survived of purely Greek activities came
to them by direct descent, they were also the heirs of all that
Rome had given to the world.   As her dominion and empire
expanded, one area after another had been brought under her
influence; everywhere the Roman administration had been
planted, and Roman Law had been enforced.   Of all this
marvellous mechanism of government Constantinople became

[1] It was the closest approximation that Europe has afforded to the
condition which Mill describes as the Stationary State. *Political Economy*,
bk. IV. c. 6.

[2] Bury, *op. cit.* I. 100, 338.

[3] On this most interesting monument of the time compare Lethaby and
Swainson, *The Church of S. Sophia.*

the new centre ; she was the home of the imperial bureaucracy, and it was by her lawyers that the accumulated traditions of the civil law were arranged and codified for all time. The most imperishable of all the monuments of Justinian's reign is that code of Civil Law, which preserves a model to be copied universally by magistrates and legislators in doing even-handed justice. But even that which was most characteristically Latin was modified when it was recast into its final form; the system of government under Justinian was derived from that which had been created by Octavius, but its character was entirely changed. The influence of the Church in the East had at length awakened a strong sense of nationality among the Greeks[1]; and the Byzantine imperialism, by infusing oriental forms with this new Greek spirit, brought about the long-deferred realisation of the policy of Alexander the Great.

There was no department of secular life in which the citizens of Constantinople did not, as a community, enjoy the best that the world had brought to birth ; and it was a great advantage to the Greeks that they had adopted the noblest faith which man has known. Apart altogether from the hopes it gave and the ideals it put before them, there were direct material effects of Christianity which made it beneficial. There was a more eager effort than before to deal with the problems of poverty, and to lighten the lot of the slave[2], while the enforcement of the Sunday rest was a gain to every class of workers. It is not indeed in the East that the full influence of Christianity on economic life can be assessed; that is most clearly seen in the West, where the disconnected fragments of Imperial society were eventually reconstructed under Christian influence and on a Christian basis.

[1] Finlay, I. 133.

[2] Though Christianity certainly discouraged slavery and lessened its evils, "the economical conditions which changed the slave system into the colonate and serf system were the chief cause" of improvement. Bury, *op. cit.* I. p. 370.

For after all, though Constantinople was from the first a Christian town, with Christian rather than pagan temples and worship, it showed in many ways that the highly developed civilization it contained had been Christianised but was not Christian in its origin. The place which the Emperor held in ecclesiastical affairs was natural enough in the political descendant of a ruler who had been the chief of the priestly college. The games of the circus, and the factions to which they gave rise, were natural enough in a new Rome, where the traditions of old Rome were maintained without a break; they were not organised anew in the older city when it rose from the ruins to which it had been reduced by the Goths. Even the code of Civil Law, though the Christian influence is clear enough in parts, retains much that shows that the leaven had not worked very thoroughly; the subsequent conflicts between the Civilians and the Canonists indicate the manner in which, in its conceptions of property and of marriage, the Civil Law was fundamentally at variance with Christian teaching.

The civilization of Constantinople, then, contained little new development of any kind, but just because there was so little in it that was fresh or original, it may all the more fittingly be regarded as the store-house in which all that was best in previous attainments was preserved till the times changed, and the new nations were ready to receive the treasure that had been kept in store for them.

70. There is one department of life in regard to which the service rendered by Constantinople to modern Europe is adequately recognised. It is, indeed, *Links of connection with the West.* too patent to be ignored. At the fall of Constantinople there was a sudden emigration of Greek scholars with Greek manuscripts to Italy, and the impulse which was given to literary studies found its natural result in the Renascence. From that time the literature and philosophy and theology of modern Europe may fitly be dated. The era when the wealth of classical literature, which had been

preserved at Constantinople, was brought within the reach of Italian scholarship, is rightly spoken of as the revival of learning; it was the revival of knowledge that had once existed, but had long before perished, in the West, though it survived in the East.

It is not sufficiently remembered, however, that this was but the last and most striking example of a process which had been going on indirectly and gradually for centuries. Civilization was communicated by roundabout and devious paths, but none the less is it true that Western Europe had little to boast of but what it had received directly or indirectly from Constantinople. We look back on the thirteenth century in particular as a period of extraordinary intellectual activity in many directions, both literary and legal, philosophical and scientific. The habits of thought, which were then diffused, turned men's minds towards the cultivation of empirical science; and the elements of chemistry and of medicine were being disseminated by Jewish practitioners in many cities of the West. Astronomy too was cultivated, and there was a remarkable outburst of theological study in the effort to reconcile this new knowledge with the Christian verities. The new interest in empirical science and the new philosophy which dealt with it, were both derived from Spain, where they had flourished at Cordova under the protecting influence of the Caliphs: but neither one nor the other was of Arabian origin. The Arabs originated little or nothing; they acquired much, they carried it with them, and they were the agents of its redistribution through Western Europe. But their science was Greek, their medicine was Greek, their philosophy was Greek; what they had learned in the eastern provinces of the Empire, they brought by a southern route to Spain; and thence, this new knowledge, reversing the course of the barbarian conquest, made its way to central and northern Europe.

The revival of the study of Roman Law in the thirteenth century was hardly second in importance to the intellectual impulse which was communicated through Arabian channels. But it bore on its face that it was not merely Roman Law; the *Corpus Juris Civilis* consisted of Roman Law as modified and codified in the East; the very names of Theodosius and Justinian take us back, not to Rome, but to Constantinople.

There was another contemporary change in Europe which marks the dawn of the reviving life in Western cities. It is a commonplace to speak of the Crusades as opening up an extraordinary amount of commercial activity, which led to the formation and the freeing of numberless towns. That too seems to be a Latin movement, preached by a Latin monk and encouraged by the Latin Pontiff. But though the initiative came from the West, the solid fruits were gathered from the East. Western Christendom came in contact with the glories of Constantinople and the flourishing cities of Syria. In so far as the Venetians and Genoese were enabled to lay the foundations of their commercial greatness at this epoch, they did it by securing a firm footing in ˙Constantinople and in the regions to which Constantinople gave them access.

To trace the full indebtedness of Western Europe to Constantinople it would be necessary to follow the history of industrial and commercial development through mediæval to modern times; it may suffice here to have pointed out thus briefly the more obvious instances of obligations under which we lie to the Byzantine Greeks. But it should not be forgotten that the heritage which has been transmitted to us also includes many elements which we owe to ancient Greece, and that these are not the less real because they lie so deeply hidden. When we remember how thoroughly the commercial habits of republican Rome were impregnated with Greek influence, and how many Greek colonies were included as members in the Roman Empire, we may feel that we have thought too much of the hands that reached out to us the gifts of civilization, and have not duly honoured the gracious mother from whom they were sent.

The columns in this chronological chart represent the duration of different polities which have made important economic contributions to Western Civilization. In the columns beginning or ending in a point, the gradual growth or decline from a given time is indicated. The horizontal lines show periods of expansion or influence, and the arrowheads give the direction thereof (→ east, ← west). The economic unity of the Roman Empire is indicated by a cross band. The blank columns represent Semitic, the shaded ones Aryan, polities.

CHRONOLOGICAL CHART.

Western Civilization in its Economic Aspects

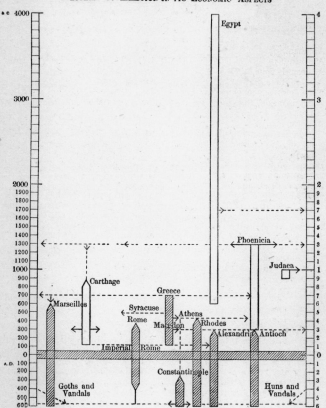

INDEX.

CAMBRIDGE HISTORICAL SERIES

Edited by G. W. PROTHERO, Litt.D., LL.D., Honorary Fellow
of King's College, Cambridge and formerly Professor of
History in the University of Edinburgh.

The Volumes already published are indicated by an
asterisk, those not so marked are in hand, for which orders
are registered, and others will be added from time to time.

*1. The French Monarchy, 1483—1789. By A. J.
GRANT, M.A., Professor of History in the University, Leeds. With
4 Maps. In 2 vols. Second Edition. 7/- net.

2. Germany and the Empire, 1493—1792. By
A. F. POLLARD, M.A., Professor of History in University College,
London.

*3. Italy from 1494 to 1790. By Mrs H. M. VERNON
(K. Dorothea Ewart). With 4 maps. Crown 8vo. 5/6 net.

*4. Spain; its greatness and decay, 1479—1788.
By Major MARTIN A. S. HUME. With an Introduction by EDWARD
ARMSTRONG, M.A., Fellow of Queen's College, Oxford. With
2 Maps. Second Edition. 4/6 net.

*5. Slavonic Europe. A Political History of Poland
and Russia from 1447 to 1796. By R. NISBET BAIN. 5/6 net.

*6. The Revolutionary and Napoleonic Era, 1789
—1815. By J. HOLLAND ROSE, Litt.D. With 6 Maps and Plans.
Sixth Edition revised. 3/6 net.

7. Modern France, 1815—1900.

8. Modern Germany, 1815—1889.

*9. The Union of Italy, 1815—1895. By W. J.
STILLMAN, L.H.D., formerly "Times" correspondent in Rome.
With 4 Maps. New Edition, revised, with an Epilogue by G. M.
Trevelyan. 4/6 net.

5000 : 11. 09.

*25. Outlines of English Industrial History. By
W. CUNNINGHAM, D.D., Fellow of Trinity College, Cambridge,
and ELLEN A. MᶜARTHUR, Lecturer at Girton College. Crown 8vo.
Third Edition. 3/- net.

*26. An Essay on Western Civilization in its Eco-
nomic Aspects. By W. CUNNINGHAM, D.D. Crown 8vo. Vol. I.
Ancient Times. With 5 Maps. Vol. II. Mediaeval and Modern
Times. With 3 Maps. 3/6 net each vol.

Extracts from the Reviews

Mr R. Nisbet Bain's "Slavonic Europe"

The Spectator.—"Mr R. Nisbet Bain has given us a book which was
long wanted....Much of the history of Eastern Europe is still unexplored;
and we cannot give Mr Bain's work higher praise than to say that out of
the tangle he has produced a singularly compact, clear, and well-pro-
portioned history that ought to be a safe and welcome guide to thousands
of readers."

Sir J. G. Bourinot's "Canada"

Daily Chronicle.—"It would scarcely be possible to find a man in the
Dominion better suited to play the part of its historian than the author of
this volume....As a textbook of Canadian history Sir John Bourinot's work
is admirable."

Prof. Hume Brown's "History of Scotland"

The Athenæum.—"The promise of Prof. Hume Brown's first volume is
more than fulfilled in the second. The author's thorough knowledge of
the sources, his gift of lucid condensation, and fine sense of proportion
have made this comparatively short work the most complete and satis-
factory history of Scotland which we possess. His pages are not over-
crowded with details, and the reader's interest is secured from beginning
to end by the admirable way in which he is led to find, in the conflict
of political and social forces, the gradual evolution of the national
destiny."

Dr Cunningham's "Western Civilization" &c.

The Athenæum.—"One of the most important portions of the equipment of the student of economics. They are not merely storehouses of
trustworthy and wide-ranging fact, of lucid and stimulating generalization,
they are a trenchant blow struck in the long strife over the method of
economics....The sweep and scope of the work are immense."

Sir R. K. Douglas's "Europe and the Far East"

The Daily News.—"This volume of the Cambridge Historical Series
possesses the same mark of excellence that has distinguished its predecessors. It is written by an expert familiar with every branch of the
subject; it is loaded with facts presented indeed in a luminous and orderly
fashion."

[*Turn over*

Cambridge Historical Series

Prof. Grant's " French Monarchy"

The Spectator.—"This is a clear, thoughtful, readable, and most useful history of the Monarchy in France, from the consolidation of its power under Louis XI to the many causes of its downfall with Louis XVI."

Major Hume's "Spain"

The Speaker.—"Major Hume's volume is in all respects worthy of the great reputation which he has won as an expert in the domain of Spanish history....Major Hume's knowledge is as complete as possible, and to a perfect mastery of his material he adds an impartiality and luminous insight which are exceedingly rare....His wide and deep acquaintance with the immense literature of his subject, his singular grasp of detail, and his cold lucidity have enabled him to present us with an historical handbook, convincing, brilliant and final in its kind. This is no dry chronicle, but a vivid and picturesque transcript of events."

Sir H. H. Johnston's "Africa"

The Times.—"Sir Harry Johnston has devoted both industry and ability to its performance, and deserves the thanks of future students for the result. This history...presents within handy compass an extremely valuable expanded index of African history as a whole....As a textbook of African study his book supplies a want which has been generally felt, and should be in proportion warmly welcomed."

Mr F. H. Skrine's "The Expansion of Russia"

The Pall Mall Gazette.—"The best account yet printed in England of the growth of Russia during the last century....This book will not only be useful to the general reader, but it forms a handy reference-book which any student of the Eastern Question will be glad to have within easy reach."

Dr Stillman's "Union of Italy"

The Times.—"Few men are better qualified by personal knowledge, by political sympathies, or by direct contact with events than Mr W. J. Stillman to write a history of modern Italy....His volume is, especially in its later chapters, a history largely written from sources of knowledge not yet fully accessible to the outside world."

Mrs H. M. Vernon's "Italy from 1494 to 1790"

The Inquirer.—"Mrs Vernon has performed her task with infinite skill, and few historical writers could have given us such a wide survey of the political, commercial, and artistic life of the Italian people in the period under discussion, while at the same time condensing the facts and preserving the continuity of the theme."

CAMBRIDGE UNIVERSITY PRESS
LONDON: FETTER LANE
C. F. CLAY, Manager
EDINBURGH: 100, PRINCES STREET

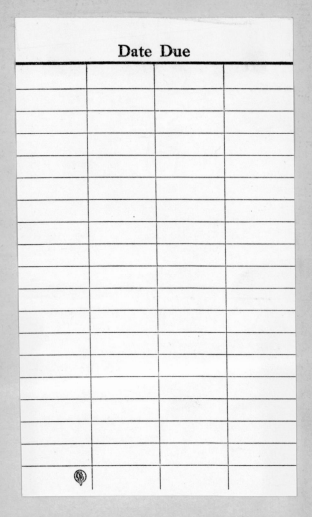

Date Due